D0606444

The English Country Town

The English Country Town

Anthony Quiney
Photographs by Robin Morrison

With 320 color illustrations

Thames and Hudson

For P. and B.

Half-title: Shops in Arundel, West Sussex.
Titlepage: Chipping Campden, Gloucestershire, from the west.

Any copy of this book issued by the publisher as a paperback is sold subject to the condition that it shall not by way of trade or otherwise be lent, resold, hired out or otherwise circulated without the publisher's prior consent in any form of binding or cover other than that in which it is published and without a similar condition including these words being imposed on a subsequent purchaser.

© 1987 Thames and Hudson Ltd, London

First published in the United States in 1987 by
Thames and Hudson Inc., 500 Fifth Avenue,
New York, New York 10110

Library of Congress Catalog Card Number 86-51165

Map: Hanni Bailey

All Rights Reserved. No part of this publication may be reproduced or transmitted in any form or by any means, electronic or mechanical, including photocopy, recording or any other information storage and retrieval system, without prior permission in writing from the publisher.

Printed and bound in Hong Kong

Contents

The Garden Counties

Arundel,
  West Sussex
Farnham,
  Surrey
Faversham,
  Kent
Lewes,
  East Sussex
Midhurst,
  West Sussex
Rye,
  East Sussex
Sandwich,
  Kent
Tunbridge Wells,
  Kent
Windsor,
  Berkshire

The West Country

Barnstaple,
  Devon
Blandford Forum,
  Dorset
Bradford-on-Avon,
  Wiltshire
Dorchester,
  Dorset
Glastonbury,
  Somerset
Malmesbury,
  Wiltshire
Marlborough,
  Wiltshire
Shaftesbury,
  Dorset
Sherborne,
  Dorset
Tavistock,
  Devon
Tiverton,
  Devon
Totnes,
  Devon

The Heart of England

Burford,
  Oxfordshire
Chipping Campden,
  Gloucestershire
Cirencester,
  Gloucestershire
Great Malvern,
  Hereford and Worcester
Ledbury,
  Hereford and Worcester
Ludlow,
  Shropshire
Much Wenlock,
  Shropshire
Ross-on-Wye,
  Hereford and Worcester
Shrewsbury,
  Shropshire
Stratford-upon-Avon,
  Warwickshire
Tewkesbury,
  Gloucestershire
Warwick,
  Warwickshire

Lakeland and the Peaks

Appleby,
  Cumbria
Bakewell,
  Derbyshire
Buxton,
  Derbyshire
Keswick,
  Cumbria
Kirkby Lonsdale,
  Cumbria
Settle,
  North Yorkshire

Castles and Dales

Alnwick,
  Northumberland
Barnard Castle,
  Durham
Beverley,
  Humberside
Harrogate,
  North Yorkshire
Helmsley,
  North Yorkshire
Hexham,
  Northumberland
Knaresborough,
  North Yorkshire
Richmond,
  North Yorkshire

In the Eastern Realms

Aylsham,
  Norfolk
Bury St Edmunds,
  Suffolk
Louth,
  Lincolnshire
Oundle,
  Northamptonshire
Saffron Walden,
  Essex
Stamford,
  Lincolnshire
Swaffham,
  Norfolk
Wisbech,
  Cambridgeshire

SCOTLAND

WALES

ENGLAND

Alnwick

Hexham

Keswick

Barnard Castle

Appleby

Richmond

Kirkby Lonsdale

Helmsley

Settle

Knaresborough
Harrogate

Beverley

Buxton

Bakewell

Louth

Shrewsbury

Aylsham

Much Wenlock

Stamford

Wisbech

Swaffham

Ludlow

Oundle

Warwick

Bury St Edmunds

Great Malvern

Stratford-upon-Avon

Ledbury

Chipping Campden

Saffron Walden

Tewkesbury

Ross-on-Wye

Burford

Cirencester

Malmesbury

LONDON

Marlborough

Windsor

Bradford-on-Avon

Faversham

Sandwich

Barnstaple

Glastonbury

Shaftesbury

Farnham

Tunbridge Wells

Tiverton

Sherborne

Midhurst

Rye

Blandford Forum

Arundel

Lewes

Dorchester

Tavistock

Totnes

0   60 Miles
0   100 Km

N

The Shakespeare Hostelrie in Stratford-upon-Avon (RIGHT), next to the Georgian town hall, and the view of Great Malvern from the heights of the Malvern Hills that Edward Elgar knew (BELOW) are both full of associations. The two scenes may have affected Shakespeare and Elgar in their different ways, but otherwise have little to do with them. More to the point is the expressive way the close-set timbers in Stratford demonstrate the wealth of the town's burgesses in the 16th century, which incidentally helped to pay for Shakespeare's education at the local grammar school. Similarly the windswept Malvern Hills sheltered a priory long before the newly married Elgar came to live here and found inspiration in this corner of the land.

English Country Towns and their History

'GOD made the country, and man made the town.' So said the poet William Cowper in 1783. Yet even by his day, the face of the countryside had already been heavily touched by man, while towns, though man's creation, depended in the first instance on the topography and the natural resources of the land around them.

Towns were nevertheless always a vital stage removed from man's fight to subsist, and over the years have become far more than that. They are one of the most complex creations of civilization and lie at the heart of every nation's cultural heritage. They do this on two levels: on the surface and deep in their character. Stratford-upon-Avon is synonymous with Shakespeare, and one cannot think of Great Malvern without Edward Elgar springing to mind, or Dorchester without Thomas Hardy. But those towns mean more than their associations with diverse talents of that sort. They were not so much created by artists as by countless individuals, most of them anonymous. The handful of celebrities who happened to live in them often made them famous, but the towns would be much the same if the celebrities had never existed.

English towns, like those of other countries, have a character of their own that distinctly belongs to the land from which they spring as well as to the people who made them. You would not mistake Alnwick for Aachen, nor Burford for Blois. Their Englishness sets them apart from the German and French qualities of their Continental counterparts. None the less there is hardly one basic feature in the make-up of English towns that is not an importation. These features include such things as the imposition of a regular plan of streets, the provision of a market place, and the influence of an adjoining monastery or castle. Though these features are common to many towns, the environment steps in and so do the people who mould it, giving each town a distinct character of its own. That is why Alnwick and Burford, Stratford and Dorchester have grown so differently in the English landscape.

If you peel back that growth and, with it, the accretions of time, it is often possible to discover the particular basic features of a town that brought it into being in the first place. They were designed to satisfy a number of special needs beyond merely domestic ones, and it is this that differentiates towns from villages. These needs might be military, economic, administrative or religious, and several of them usually combined to give birth to most towns. It is in the way they fulfil these needs that country towns differ from villages, for, while villages can satisfy many of these needs, a town does so in a more substantial way, and, in doing so, spreads its influence far beyond its immediate boundaries. Similarly country towns can be distinguished from the more important industrial towns and regional capitals because they have not entirely outgrown their origins.

The origins of towns

Many towns needed the protection of a castle and some grew up in their shadow. Totnes was already two or three hundred years old when its castle was built (LEFT). It is typical of early castles in having a conical earthen motte surrounded by a flat bailey. Its timber tower was soon replaced by a stone shell-keep with an embattled parapet, but the original form is still clearly visible here. The monasteries were an earlier influence on the development of towns than castles, and they have changed even more. Though their churches sometimes survived the Dissolution, the rest of the abbey buildings usually fell into ruins, as at Bury St Edmunds (BOTTOM LEFT). This has obscured the economic role that they played, leaving the great monastic barns such as the one at Bradford-on-Avon as a sole reminder of their wealth (see page 63).

Both castle and monastery ultimately depended on money. Some of it might come from the collection of taxes, more through charging rents on their land. But there was always more still to be obtained by sending the produce of their estates to market. This market therefore assumed a central role in a town's commercial life, and needed to be fostered by castle or monastery, sometimes by the symbolic provision of a market cross. These developed into Market Halls, such as the one at Ross-on-Wye (ABOVE), and provided shelter for the traders as well as a continuing symbol of a town's commercial prosperity. In the hall above the open arcades burgesses settled all matters affecting trade.

As commercial success brought a town's burgesses more power, they eventually came to run not just trade but all their town's affairs themselves and turned market houses into town halls. Windsor's Market Hall (1689) became the administrative centre of the town as well as a centre of commerce (RIGHT).

No town can survive without water, and rivers were the most significant topographical feature to determine the siting of nearly every town. The confluence of the Rivers Derwent and Cocker gave Cockermouth a fine defensible site for a castle and a means of transport without being too wide for a bridge (BELOW). This brought the town into being as well as giving it its name, but the water also serves a brewery at Cockermouth and so caters for an older need still, man's thirst.

The origin of towns lies in prehistory with the founding of Jericho in the 7th millennium BC, but in England the first real towns arrived just within the opening phase of its history. They were Roman creations, and, that far, they were importations. The Romans gave them what they gave all towns: walls and forts for defence; markets, shops and warehouses for manufacturing and commerce; basilicas and public squares for administration; temples and shrines for religion; baths and theatres for entertainment, as well as houses for the inhabitants. And they did all this within the confines of carefully laid-out plans that imposed order on their buildings and put them into an easily comprehensible context.

Nevertheless their first concern was a good water supply. The Romans appreciated that clear, fresh water was synonymous with health, and the aqueducts that stride across the landscape to their drier towns are one of their characteristic trademarks. In Britain, however, water was at hand nearly everywhere. Although a spring, a well or even a pond might be enough to serve a village, for a town a river was almost a necessity. This was not just because more people drank more water, but because a river served so much more than thirst. Indeed rivers had to serve many of those needs that were particular to towns, whether military, economic or even administrative.

Most English country towns were founded in the thousand years between the departure of the Romans in 410 and the end of the Middle Ages. It was a period of invasion, conflict and general mayhem. Towns therefore had to be defended, and, because towns could be defended, they were often founded as strongholds on strategic sites to defend the surrounding countryside. Such towns were called *burhs*. In the later 9th century King Alfred founded a large number of *burhs* as a means of defending Wessex from the incursions of the Danes. The Danes similarly founded *burhs*, among them the Five Boroughs of the Danelaw, the part of the Midlands that fell under Danish rule. After 1066 William the Conqueror and his noblemen, above all the powerful Roger de Montgomery, founded castles with towns in their shadow, to control the land. The best sites for these towns were those where, as at Ludlow, there was a hill almost surrounded by a bend in a river.

While a river aided defence, it might also make defence imperative, for instance where it forced its course through a range of hills and provided an easy route for invaders. Lewes started as a Saxon *burh* to defend the gap where the Sussex Ouse cuts through the South Downs, and the Normans built a castle here to strengthen the defences of both the town and this route.

Rivers were even more important economically. They promoted trade, because long-distance transport was far better served by boat than by cart. The Roman port of Clausentum on the River Itchen was superseded by the Saxon Hamwic, founded across the river about 721 by King Ine, and, after Viking raids, refounded on a low hill overlooking the River Test as Southampton. Many smaller ports were sited inland on navigable rivers, like Stratford-upon-Avon, so important was water transport.

Nearly every town founded beside a river needed a crossing and that usually meant a bridge. Sometimes the bridge came first and made the town a centre of communications, bringing custom from travellers who had no other purpose than to pass through. A really well-connected town might become more than a centre of communications and assume the role of an administrative centre for the region, as Stamford did in the Danelaw. When the administration of the country had been strengthened and formalized by the Normans, good communications between administrative centres became essential. For example Shrewsbury had the River Severn to give access up and down the length of the west Midlands, and two bridges across the river leading to London one way and to Wales the other. Shrewsbury consequently was ideally sited to become the county town of Shropshire.

Rivers were crucial to the economy of towns in other ways than transport and communications, and never more so than by serving manufacture. Until the middle of the 14th century England's major export was wool. Thereafter, weaving rapidly expanded and the country's major export became cloth. It produced more wealth in England than anything else. In fact the need to produce cloth in ever greater quantities and ever more cheaply gave the Industrial Revolution much of its impetus. Long before that, cloth had given countless country towns, especially those on the wetter, western side of the country, the wealth that made them great. The reason is that cloth manufacture needs the vast quantities of clear water that many western towns had in abundance. Spinning, weaving, dyeing, fulling and finishing all require it, and from the later Middle Ages fast-moving streams were also used to provide power for fulling mills by means of waterwheels. Water, therefore, served many of a town's needs as well as the most essential.

The Romans chose the sites of their British towns with care, and gave them buildings as sophisticated in construction as they were specialized in use. Sadly, little of this survived the collapse of the Empire at the start of the 5th century. Writing a century and a half later, the English historian Gildas mourned the loss of those towns. They had been the most overt sign of Roman civilization, and they survived only in the imagination to inspire the future.

Most Roman towns were nevertheless reborn after a lapse of a century or two, but in a different guise and with far poorer buildings. Corinium became Cirencester, though as a shadow of its former self and no longer the capital of the West Country. Bristol took this role because, in the new conditions, a port for trade was more useful than an administrative centre at the junction of roads laid out for the use of imperial armies.

While Roman towns were remade, new towns were born. By the 8th century English agriculture was again producing surpluses that could support extensive manufacture and trade. Hamwic had at least five thousand inhabitants, making it the most populous town of its day so far discovered in Europe. An infrastructure of workshops, warehouses, markets and ports was back in business.

While agriculture needed towns for the marketing and processing of its products, it gained much of its impetus for improvement from the monasteries that were founded by early missionaries in the 6th and 7th centuries, and by the greater wave of foundations that followed the Norman Conquest. Many monasteries tempted towns to spring up outside their gates, as perhaps the abbey did at Glastonbury after its foundation about 700, and William the Conqueror's Battle Abbey certainly did. As an owner of well-exploited estates, an abbey was a great producer of goods. As a centre of population and culture, it was also a consumer and a centre of hospitality. All this promoted trade. Some abbey churches also became cathedrals and an even greater incentive to growth (the special story of ancient cathedral towns is outside the scope of this book). Some orders of monks preferred to keep away from the temptations of the world. The Cistercians, for instance, were disinclined to let towns spring up at their gates. So, while the Benedictine Tewkesbury Abbey was part of the town, the Cistercian Rievaulx remained secluded and the town that served it, Helmsley, grew up a respectful distance away.

A castle could similarly give a town its first impetus and bring it continuing economic benefits. Castles were Norman importations that were

The landscape of towns

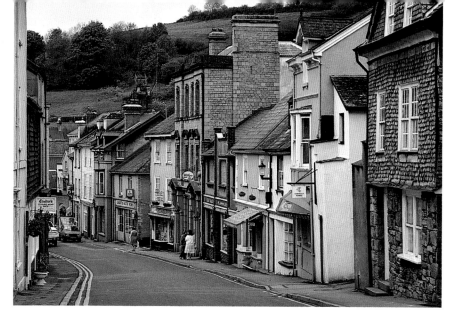

The constantly changing appearance of a town depends as much on the spaces between its buildings as on the buildings themselves. This is invariably true of towns that have grown in piecemeal fashion, but it is also true of planned towns. The grid of streets chosen by many early planners may tend to produce a monotonous effect, but this is offset by the streets themselves, which often widen to form a market place or suddenly become confined by an entrance gate. This happens in the planned town of Ludlow, and again at the less formal Beverley where North Bar (TOP LEFT) effectively terminates the street before it leads out of the town.

The contrast between wide main streets and narrow alleys can be found in any country town, and never better than at Tewkesbury (see the two views BOTTOM LEFT). This was the result of a town having to make the best use of a confined site, and laying out three main streets that centred on a small market place. These were the only wide streets, and they left every other route as a mere passageway hemmed in by buildings.

All towns prize open spaces. They might be no more than a churchyard, but sometimes they are the wider spaces surrounding a former abbey or enclosed by the bailey walls of a castle. A few towns were lucky in maintaining common land or having generous landowners who gave land on the understanding that it remained open. Ross-on-Wye had the benefit of an unusually generous private citizen who gave the town a small park called the Prospect (see page 113). By the 18th century such parks were desirable features of any town and some mitigation for increasing size and concentration of building. This was unimportant in a small town like Ashburton (TOP RIGHT) where the surrounding countryside is never out of sight, but in Harrogate (CENTRE RIGHT) there are great swathes of inalienable common land that stretch right to the town centre, much to its benefit.

The range of architectural styles as well as the various forms of building that define open spaces can drastically alter the effect of an open space, regardless of its size. The ragged form of the varied houses in West Street, Ashburton (TOP RIGHT), produces a quite different effect from the lively but nevertheless ordered shape of the terraces of Tunbridge Wells (BOTTOM RIGHT).

built especially as a means of establishing political control. Their function, therefore, was administrative and domestic as well as military. So a castle had to provide accommodation for its lord, who held his power from the king and wielded it over the area under his control. Above all this meant a great room or hall for discussing public matters and trying legal cases, and lesser rooms for keeping records, holding prisoners, accommodating guests and servants as well as guards and a garrison, and for keeping the whole establishment well stocked with food and other provisions.

The first castles were built of earth and timber. They comprised a 'motte' or mound of earth with a timber tower on the top, and an adjoining 'bailey' – a large open space for subsidiary buildings, defended by an embanked palisade. By the 12th century many of these early castles were being rebuilt in stone with more elaborate accommodation as the wealth of the lord allowed. Since that wealth came from his estates, he would be keen to develop them and encourage whatever trade they brought in their wake. So castles often helped towns to grow up in their shadow. Some castles became provincial centres of administration, as Lewes Castle became the centre from which the county of Sussex was governed. Eventually the castle fell out of use, but Lewes remained the county town of Sussex, and the functions of the castle were transferred to separate, more modern, buildings, such as the County Hall, Record Office and Jail. This could bring prosperity to a town that would thrive only meagrely if left to a market for local produce.

Trade and manufacturing, even so, were vital to the success of most towns. By the time of the Norman Conquest, the former *burhs* of Wessex and the Danelaw were now called boroughs and several other places achieved borough status by obtaining charters to establish their rights to hold weekly markets or annual fairs, or to mint coins. A charter would give their citizens or burgesses a degree of self-government and freedom from the obligations of villagers to serve their local lord. In return burgesses paid rent on the land they occupied to the overlord of the borough, who might be the king, the abbot of a local monastery or the lord of the castle. The burgesses soon formed a rising middle class of merchants and manufacturers on a par with the free yeomen of the countryside. They joined together into a variety of corporate bodies, such as guilds, to regulate their affairs, especially entry into their particular trades or crafts, and to administer markets and fairs and other matters relating to trade and manufacture. The Church had a hand in this, as it always did in the Middle Ages, providing its blessing and authority and gaining financially from endowments and other gifts, if not from rents as well. Meanwhile the landlord did his utmost to see the town flourish, as his rents depended on it.

Increasingly the market place and its buildings dominated the life of the town, and became its economic hub where burgesses gathered to do business. The castle or monastery took a back seat. By the 15th century castles had lost most of their military value anyway, though they remained important as residences and administrative centres for a while. More importantly, by the 1540s Henry VIII's Dissolution of the Monasteries had suppressed hundreds of religious institutions and their wealth was redistributed. Towns had to do without them, and many did very well indeed.

The growing power of burgesses is apparent in the buildings of the market place. The smallest markets were given a cross, a symbol of piety and the partnership between the Church and trade, but a more prosperous market, such as the one at Malmesbury, might have an elaborate, open building that could shelter a few tradesmen (see page 71). These were still called market crosses or sometimes butter or poultry crosses after the principal goods sold within them. A far more useful form of building was increasingly favoured as the influence of the Church waned and was then abolished. This comprised an arcaded ground floor, and a larger chamber above. The ground floor was simply an enlargement of the space within a market cross, but the upper chamber was an innovation. It contained a hall where the burgesses of the particular guild that ran the market could meet, and at the same time it gave them an object of civic pride.

As towns developed, burgesses increasingly became involved in running the town's affairs. So the market hall was used for wider and wider purposes. These extended ever further beyond the running of the market, the regulation of trade and purely commercial considerations, to the running of the whole of the town's affairs. The market hall in effect became the town hall and took on all the various roles of accommodating the town's local government. Some market halls, for instance those at Windsor and Bury St Edmunds, started life as the Market Hall and actually changed their names to the Town Hall. Others that had the grander name of Guildhall continued with it when the guilds that ran them successfully severed their connection with the Church at the time of the Dissolution, and continued as purely secular institutions.

The secularization of the country town with the progressive reduction in the influence of the Church had other results that show in its building history. Monasteries were responsible for most of the social welfare of medieval England. They provided accommodation for pilgrims and travellers, hospitals to shelter the poor, the sick and the aged, and colleges and schools to educate people in Latin and Greek so as to enable them to enter Holy Orders. The Church was also responsible for the founding of the first universities. Many of these burdens were already being shouldered by burgesses before the Dissolution. They founded almshouses to shelter the aged poor. They founded new schools to teach English grammar and mathematics, and subsidized their fees. Many of these grammar schools have lasted until the present, either independent (though their fees have risen), or incorporated into the state system of education and free. Yet others took the path of some former Church schools in the 19th century and were reformed as public schools where fee-paying and an emphasis on Latin and Greek ironically helped to make them bastions of privilege rather than either fully public or free.

Inns shook themselves loose from the Church's control and became one of the English country town's most cherished institutions, where liquor and conversation nourish each other, and the monastic guest house became the town hotel, usually placed to overlook the market where travellers would most need it. As for the monastery's buildings, they were taken down piecemeal, their materials dispersed to new building works or converted to new uses. If the burgesses saw fit to buy it, the monastic church escaped to become a new, grand parish church and to continue to adorn their town.

Towns often grew up around their main buildings, and then expanded along lines of least resistance such as the roads leading out into the countryside and the secondary streets and lanes running between them. Sometimes new streets or quarters were specially planned instead. Farnham grew up along the ancient highway between London and Winchester, but its market was specially planned in a new, wide street, which the Bishop of Winchester as landlord laid out between the old thoroughfare and his castle. At Chipping Campden, the new wealth brought by the cloth trade gave the town a brand new curving main street, again wide enough for a market. It ignored the old village, leaving the church and manor behind the High Street, almost

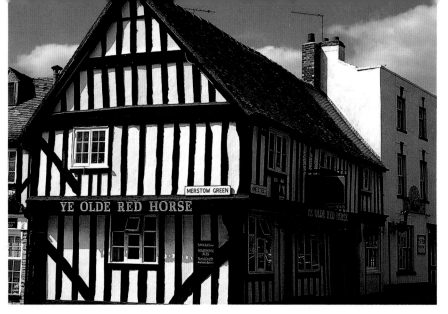

Building materials

*The Bradford-on-Avon barn (*CENTRE LEFT*) is
made from fine oölitic limestone, an easily
cut, hard-wearing stone that weathers far
better than the Triassic sandstones of the
Midlands used at Ross-on-Wye (*ABOVE*). The
hard Carboniferous stones of the Pennines
and the red sandstones of the Eden valley, as
seen together in Appleby (*BOTTOM RIGHT*),
equally resist the chisel and the harsh
weather. Where stone was lacking, there was
often clay. It favoured the growth of oak for
timber framing, for instance around Evesham
(*TOP LEFT*), and made the tiles of Midhurst
(*TOP*) and the bricks of Wisbech (*BOTTOM
LEFT*).*

In the late 18th century the obsolescent timber frame was re-created in iron and a century later in steel. The iron frame had many advantages over timber. It was stronger and could be easily mass-produced in a greater variety of shapes. Consequently it could serve in a greater variety of forms, as the dome built over the former stables at Buxton (ABOVE) shows. Nevertheless iron is not entirely fireproof and steel additionally suffers from rust, and in some ways both need more maintenance than timber, so whether they will last as long is still open to question.

Commercial Life

Towns depend on commerce for their wealth. It is therefore hardly surprising, in view of the English climate, that enclosed shops have partly superseded open markets. Workshops go back to prehistoric times and no doubt doubled as places for the sale of goods as they did in the Middle Ages. The combination of a place to make goods and a place to display them was all that a medieval shop needed, and today things are not so different, however sophisticated the processes of manufacture, storage and sale have become.

The timber-framed shops in Sandwich (BOTTOM LEFT) no longer contain shops as simple as those of the 16th century when they were built, but the shop windows only replace simpler display counters, set back from unglazed openings in the same place. The old-fashioned display TOP LEFT is Victorian in character, but, the mirrors apart, probably not so different from a late medieval display.

The Romans had shopping arcades, but the arcade in England, like the one at Okehampton (TOP CENTRE), was a progressive adaptation of medieval forms. It had its heyday in the 19th century when cheap glass and iron made it into an internal shopping street, lit from above. This was an improvement on the traditional half-open covered arcade that had shops on one side and rather draughty openings on the other to let in the light.

Since the Middle Ages shops have increasingly become places for the retail sale of goods. The manufacture of goods and their wholesaling take place elsewhere in specialized buildings. Breweries, perhaps above all buildings, are no longer small rooms in houses with a counter for the sale of ale, but have reached the size of large factories. Harvey's Brewery at Lewes (TOP RIGHT) is a particularly attractive example, put up in 1880 beside the River Ouse on a site where there has been brewing continuously for at least two hundred years.

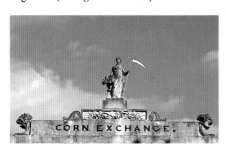

As trade grew, the sale of goods was made easier in a number of ways that took much everyday commerce away from the market place. One was to sell goods through specialized exchanges, for example the Corn Exchange at Tunbridge Wells (ABOVE). These were buildings where a wholesaler could offer samples rather than his entire produce and take the offers of the highest bidders. Transactions carried out like this increasingly took on the semblance of big business and needed the services of banks. In the 17th century most people with money worked on a system of private lending and borrowing to ease trade and paid in cash. The growth of banks in the 18th century changed all that and eventually made the payment of accounts far easier. Similarly the growth of the Post Office (RIGHT) in the 19th century made transactions over any distance easier through an efficient letter service that superseded the haphazard arrangement of sending letters between staging posts.

shut off from it, though the wealth of the town was poured into the rebuilding of the church to make it one of the finest 'wool' churches in the country.

The process of following old routes and adding new quarters wherever there was conveniently vacant land could lead to a haphazard layout. This might serve for a time, but not always for ever. On occasion a forceful landlord might decide to replan the whole town. The most sophisticated plan and at once the most drastic had a gridiron of streets on the Roman pattern. The powerful Abbot Baldwin replanned Bury St Edmunds as a grid in the 1080s, and this pattern remained common until the start of the 20th century.

Many medieval towns were surrounded by walls for their protection. The Saxon *burhs* had embanked walls crowned by palisades, but Chester and York made use of their old Roman walls when they came to build up walls again in the Middle Ages. Most stone walls, especially of towns near the sea, were added in the 14th century, often prompted by French raids. That happened at Rye, where the walls can still be traced though they are embedded in buildings. Town walls were pierced by imposing main gates or bars where the principal routes passed through them and gave a town status.

Towns were proverbially rich and people flocked to them, attracted by the prospect of quick money and an escape from the drudgery of the countryside. Such expectations were seldom completely justified, but as a town prospered, more and more people moved to it, hoping to cash in on the profits. Consequently land values rose and street frontages became even more valuable still. There was nothing to be gained by building more streets to give properties wider frontages as this would consume valuable space, nor was there invariably much to be gained by letting the town grow larger and larger. People wanted to be near the centre, and town boundaries were often strictly limited by their walls or the open fields outside. So it became common for plots to have narrow frontages, but to extend a long way backwards, perhaps to a narrow back lane. They became known as burgage plots since they were typical of towns with borough status. They can still be seen where modern rebuilding has not obscured them, for instance lining Fore Street and the High Street at Totnes.

The plot itself normally contained a main building facing the street. This might combine a house and shop, and often there would be further shops and other accommodation running down a side passage leading to a court at the rear, with further buildings lining it. Finally there could be a garden at the back, perhaps with stabling and a back lane or mews. This layout worked well up to a point, but, as land values rose, the garden and court were often progressively built over until they became the sordid rookeries of some industrial towns. In most country towns, overcrowding seldom reached these proportions, but the courts could still be cramped and unhealthy.

A large number of individual houses built in this fashion with narrow fronts and extensive building at the rear could make up a street as ordered in appearance as the streets of Totnes. More often it would produce a higgledy-piggledy appearance, picturesque to the taste of today, but chaotic in the eyes of the landlord who was concerned to get the best rents as possible. It was in his interest to exploit his holdings, so he might build more regularly and charge higher rents. By erecting a number of similar buildings, one per plot in a standard form, a regular terrace would result, and his aim might be achieved.

Early in the 14th century there were already regular terraces of standard buildings in London, and a terrace survives in Goodramgate at York that was built about 1315. The most significant terrace, both for its medieval date

Bridges

The value of a river to a town's defence and communications depended on the ease of crossing it. So important were bridges that many towns incorporated the word bridge into their names. The towns of Bradford-on-Avon (TOP RIGHT) and Stamford (BOTTOM RIGHT) suggest through their names that they started without bridges and relied on fords instead. These could be unreliable and dangerous and were always an inconvenience, however important they had once been in the choice of a site for a town. Like Barnstaple (CENTRE RIGHT), both Bradford and Stamford had built bridges by the later Middle Ages and may well have had earlier ones.

The earliest bridges were built of timber, but this rotted and could easily be swept away. To support the greater weight of a stone bridge, the mud at the bottom of a river had to be piled with timber stakes. Elm was a favourite for this as it does not readily rot when fully immersed in water. This was rather a hit-or-miss way of building, but it usually worked admirably. Later methods using modern materials started at Ironbridge in 1778-9 when the world's first large iron bridge was thrown over the River Severn near Coalbrookdale. After that all kinds of iron bridges such as lattice bridges (BOTTOM RIGHT), box-girder bridges and suspension bridges came into use, providing the 19th century with the means of making some of the finest monuments in the world. With the use of concrete, bridges today can span formidable obstacles and achieve a breath-taking beauty in the process – as well as monstrous spaghetti-like contortions in the inter-threading of motorways.

Doors

The public face of any house, or any building for that matter, is its front door. It was consequently the first part to be touched by fashion and occasionally the only part. Medieval cathedrals always made a monumental feature of their entrance doorways, filling them with carving to remind worshippers of their faith. By contrast some of the poorest industrial housing erected in the 19th century had attractive front doors even though the rest of the building was rotten to the core.

The ease with which one can exchange an old door for a new one, or a cheap door for an expensive one, is evidence of attention to fashion. Despite this, doorways can sometimes provide the best clue to a building's age and status in the world.

A house door needs to be welcoming as well as a proper barrier to strangers. It needs to preserve privacy, but not to inhibit the visitor. Discreet strength therefore must combine with an attractive surround. The surround itself provides the best opportunity for decoration. Whatever the current fashion, the material from which it is made will always be an influence. The good limestone of Chipping Campden or Oundle, for instance, allows plenty of carving, where the granite of the north and west allows practically none. Timber can be even more easily carved and, painted white, can be shown to the best advantage.

Where a doorway has a hood or porch, the difficult balance between effective shelter from rain and plenty of light needs to be achieved. This is not always an easy compromise. It was made harder especially when the door leads into a long entrance passage that had to be lit by a fanlight. An age without electricity could not rely on anything as easy as the flick of a switch.

The doors shown here come from Totnes, Rye, Chipping Campden, Bury St Edmunds and Bakewell respectively (TOP, LEFT TO RIGHT), and from Warwick (LEFT) and Oundle (RIGHT). Apart from the garden gate at Oundle, there is little difference in the actual doors, but there is much to tell the surrounds apart. The two curves of the porches at Totnes and Bakewell produce quite different effects, and there are even more differences in the various forms of classical detailing of the other surrounds. Columns and entablatures at Rye and Bury contrast with brackets and a rounded pediment at Warwick and an open pediment set on a moulded architrave at Chipping Campden. The gate at Oundle is altogether different. Its head is produced by raising the heavy moulding of the wall's parapet over the arch and the tall finials that it carries are a medieval idea carried out in the classical form of three obelisks mounted on small balls.

and wonderful state of preservation, was built in Church Street, Tewkesbury, not by the abbey itself but probably by the monks as a speculative venture in the 15th century (see page 119). This long terrace of shops and houses has a regular appearance with an effect greater than the sum of its parts. Each individual house forming the terrace occupies a vertical slice, front to back, of a two-storeyed, timber-framed building. At the front, the ground floor was given over to a shop, which could double as a workshop and a place of sale. Behind this a spiral stair led to an upper chamber, which served as a bedroom and store. The rear part of the building was a hall, a general living-room, kitchen and dining-room. A hearth was set on the floor under the open roof, which let the smoke escape.

There were a number of variations on this arrangement, both in Tewkesbury and in other medieval towns. As prosperity increased and brick or stone for a chimney-stack ceased to be a luxury beyond all but the richest, the problem of heating a terrace-house was solved. The layout of an increasing number of rooms became standardized, and the sophisticated terrace-house of the late 17th century was born. Here every house had a slice of the whole terrace, with two or more floors, and usually two rooms to each floor, one at the front and one at the back so as to make efficient use of daylight. On one side of the rooms there would be fireplaces and on the other the entrances to the rooms from the front passages, stairs and landings. This became the standard town house of later years, and even today it is still built in large numbers because, despite the introduction of modern services such as electric light, running water and main drainage, the plan is still hard to better when space and especially frontage are at a premium.

The five thousand inhabitants that filled Hamwic in the 8th century were far above the average at that time, and perhaps only five towns had so high a population by the time of the Conquest three hundred years later. Of 112 further boroughs in England maybe only ten counted populations in the thousands. The rest were in the hundreds and no more than villages by today's standards. It is hard to know how far these populations had grown by the middle of the 14th century, but, while some towns did well and others badly, on average populations probably at least doubled. Then came the Black Death, which from 1348 mercilessly gnawed its way through the teeming crowds of towns. Some towns stopped, to remain as no more than villages, though more for reasons of failing economies than failing populations. Generally towns continued to grow, so great were their attractions. Thanks above all to the cloth industry, numerous towns began to dominate the local economy. Totnes suddenly blossomed to become one of the top twenty provincial towns of England, while Beverley, which had been in the top twenty before the Black Death because of its trade in raw wool, fell into decay because it failed to profit from cloth and Hull displaced it as a port.

By the end of the 16th century England had about 760 towns. Apart from five regional centres, most country towns still had populations of only a few thousand and kept their rural character, despite flourishing trade. Two hundred years later all this had changed. Industrialization and the accompanying unprecedented growth in national population left many old towns behind. Sandwich's port silted up and the town stood still, but the cloth industry of Tiverton made the change to mill-powered machines and continued to grow, though not exorbitantly as Manchester did. So it remained a country town, and comparatively healthy since the town's principal mill owner invested in good housing for his workers.

While expanding industrial towns became more and more disease ridden, health in the form of drinking the waters of spas and bathing in them

Supplying water

The Romans brought fountains to England from the hot, dry squares of the classical world, where springs of water could be deified. In a wet country like England water is less prized than it is further south, and it has consequently always been treated publicly more for its practical uses, especially as an aid to health and cleanliness, than as a means of giving pleasure. Even water pumps as decorative as the one at Shaftesbury (ABOVE LEFT) were principally designed for use. Similarly, public fountains like those at Shrewsbury and Ludlow (BELOW, FAR LEFT AND LEFT) are often as much monuments to public benefactors concerned with health and cleanliness as objects designed to beautify towns.

became a fashionable relaxation and brought Tunbridge Wells, Great Malvern, Buxton and Harrogate into prominence. As resorts, they were a new kind of country town, the equivalent of the pilgrimage towns of the Middle Ages, but much larger. Several coastal villages expanded into seaside resorts, though these are not included here. Apart from Bath, most spas had populations of less than 10,000 in 1801, and that was true of country towns in general. Even Shrewsbury, which built the first iron-framed building in the world in 1796 to house a flax mill, just retained its character as a country town and its population did not exceed 15,000 by 1801. Most country towns, like the once dominant Stamford, turned their face entirely away from industry, and grew not at all.

They would still have been recognized by the antiquary John Leland, who described many towns in his *Itinerary* in the middle of the 16th century. The inveterate traveller, devotee of spas and commentator Celia Fiennes recorded scores of country towns between the 1680s and about 1712 in terms that still apply today. So did Daniel Defoe, the author of *Robinson Crusoe*. His *Tour Through the Whole Island of Great Britain*, published between 1724 and 1726, spoke perceptively and often caustically of many sleepy country towns and their inhabitants.

Only towards the end of the 19th century were the rewards of a quiet peaceful town first recognized widely enough to attract new inhabitants. As transport improved with the coming of the railways and then motor cars, commuters turned many a country town into a dormitory. Light industry has found these attractions too, giving some country towns much more unobtrusive factories than those that transformed the towns of the Midlands and north in the 19th century. They make hardly any demand on labour and little on space, so leaving the towns they have adopted with a new source of income but little need of change beyond a few desirable new houses. So the English country town lives on, a romantic evocation of the past and a promise for the future.

Keeping time

*In a country where only a tip of the south
coast has more than an average of five hours of
sunshine per day, it might seem futile to go to
the trouble of setting up sundials. Many of
them appear to exist not so much for showing
the time as for imparting tiresome moral
truisms such as 'Time waitethe for noe
manne'.*

*But time does indeed matter if society is to
be ordered, and ordered society is a pre-
requisite in town even if it hardly rules the
countryside. A public timepiece therefore had
its importance when most people did not carry
accurate watches. When clocks became both
common and accurate in the 17th century,
many towns built a clock tower if the parish
church could not provide a ready-built
location. A tower not only raised the clock so
all could see it, but allowed plenty of space
both for the weights that drove it by
unwinding a chain from a drum, and for a
pendulum that needed to be long if it was to be
accurate. Bells additionally gave a clock
another source of attention. A few clocks had
mechanical puppets or carillons of bells to
play the hours, but these frivolities are more
common in Germany than in England, where
clocks often maintained by their stern
upstanding towers a kind of portentousness
previously found in the inscriptions on
sundials.*

*The varied timepieces shown here are at
Launceston in Cornwall, Sherborne, Lewes
(ABOVE, LEFT TO RIGHT) and Louth (LEFT).*

The Garden Counties

BERKSHIRE
SURREY · SUSSEX
KENT

LIKE all regions of England, the south-east is an arbitrary zone that today is defined by little more than proximity to London. Before London became a great metropolis, it would have seemed absurd to group together towns, rich and poor, variously set on the flanks of the Weald of Kent, in gaps in the bare South Downs, washed by the tides of the River Thames or hard by the dry heaths of Surrey. Now they are all a quick drive from the capital, as once they could be reached by a day's ride, and that gives the region its prosperity.

It was not always like that. The ancient wealth of north Kent, for example, once contrasted with the empty wooded wilderness of the Weald to the south-west, seen here pressing up to the edge of Tunbridge Wells (*left*), and other parts of the region are similarly distinct.

As a new town, Tunbridge Wells has always depended on London for much of its existence. Most other towns in the south-east were different. Their prosperity depended on marketing the products of a varied local agriculture, and on rivers or the coast for the communications that allowed trade to flourish. Remarkably, towns seldom depended on local industries like weaving or iron-making. These were major occupations in the region, but they were undertaken in villages, sometimes even in individual farmsteads. In this corner of England there are no great churches built from the profits of the wood or iron industries, though there was plenty of wealth here by the end of the Middle Ages.

Tunbridge Wells is made of brick and timber, like all the rest of the south-east, for apart from some good Wealden sandstone and the flint that crops up in chalkland and along the coastal beaches, there is little building stone anywhere in the region. There was always plenty of timber. Oak was grown in plenty and the clay that oaks need to keep their roots damp and well nourished also produced excellent bricks, so the lack of stone was never greatly felt.

Arundel

WEST SUSSEX

*The view from Arundel Castle (*BELOW*) shows the need for defence and the advantages of the site. The mouth of the River Arun provided a safe landing for invaders as well as a harbour for boats engaged in coastal trade. The water meadows by the river were valuable grazing for cattle, and the coastal plain was rich arable land, so Arundel had a sound economic base in local agriculture as well as a secure defensive site on a spur of the South Downs overlooking the valley.*

THE view of Arundel from across the water meadows of the River Arun is among the most memorable in England, and, in its way, unusually French. The roofs of the town huddle below the towers of a castle and the tall buttresses and pinnacles of a cathedral in a way that is quite alien to the English scene.

All this is a comparatively new creation. Arundel came into prominence after the Norman Conquest because the site was exactly right to guard the river valley. Here Roger de Montgomery founded a castle with a motte and two baileys. In Henry II's reign the long process of strengthening it with strong, stone buildings began. Later, it came into the hands of the Fitzalans, Earls of Arundel, and eventually the Dukes of Norfolk. During the Civil War it was bombarded and left a ruin.

Soon after coming into his inheritance in 1860, the 15th Duke of Norfolk, a Roman Catholic, began construction of a great church in the French Gothic style. It was designed and built by the architect J. A. Hansom as a triumphant demonstration of faith, and in 1916 it became a cathedral. Then from 1890 to 1903 the Duke employed C. A. Buckler to rebuild the castle, to complete the ensemble.

The consequences of the 15th Duke of Norfolk's rebuilding of the castle and the town show at close quarters in a number of romantic views of half-timbering and crenellated towers. At the junction of High Street and Mill Road (TOP RIGHT), the past has been re-created with a seriousness that all but defeats itself. The great exception in all this revivalism is the truly ancient parish church of St Nicholas (BOTTOM RIGHT). Here the past is real, and it lives.

Much of the church was rebuilt after 1380 in the new Perpendicular style of Gothic. For example, the chancel of the church, visible here, has fine windows with perpendicular mullions running up into an ornate mass of cusped panels, the very epitome of the style.

The church was established as a college of priests, who occupied the chancel, leaving the rest for the parish. At the Dissolution of the Monasteries, such colleges were also suppressed. Here the chancel was kept as the Fitzalan chapel to contain the tombs and other monuments of the Earls of Arundel and Dukes of Norfolk. To this end it was divided by a grille from the rest of the church, which continued in parochial use. So it remained until 1880 when the vicar took the Duke of Norfolk to court, claiming ownership of the whole of the church. He lost the case and the Duke then built a brick wall to divide the Fitzalan chapel from the rest. Thankfully this has been replaced by a glass screen, but it still leaves the church uniquely divided between the Roman and the Anglican faiths.

Farnham

SURREY

BELOW: Contrasts in Castle Street. Much of it is lined by Georgian houses, glowing with red bricks set off by white-painted window frames. The oldest houses are timber framed, their fronts plastered and painted white. The most modern are comparatively ornate late Georgian and Victorian houses, built of brick in a more regular fashion, but still covered over, this time with harder stucco and again painted white.

Lower Church Lane (RIGHT), narrow, cobbled and lined by ranges of brick cottages, is a perfect foil to the church. The lower part of the tower was raised in the 15th century, but it was finished only in 1865.

FARNHAM is pre-eminently a market town. Early in the 18th century it had the greatest corn market in England, London excepted. Defoe had heard it said that once eleven hundred teams of horses drawing wagons and carts brought 44,000 bushels to Farnham's market in one day.

The town lies beside the River Wey, strung out along one main street, The Borough and its continuations East Street and West Street. These are part of the ancient highway between London and Winchester. At the centre, The Borough is crossed by two short streets, Castle Street and Church Lane. Church Lane leads down towards the parish church and the river, and Castle Street leads up towards the castle, 'nobly on a hill' as Celia Fiennes described it in 1698. The castle was begun by Henry of Blois, the brother of King Stephen, and later passed to the bishops of Winchester, who did much to stimulate the growth of the town.

There are one or two timber-framed buildings in the town, but brick houses are more numerous. The most ornate is Willmer House in West Street. It was built in 1718 with giant Doric pilasters and baroque decoration cut into the brickwork of the front, and a florid interior, readily visible to the public as the house is a museum.

The overall appearance of Farnham is Georgian, a style that aimed for a kind of uniformity and proportion in the arrangement of doors and windows, but still left plenty of room for variety as these views of Castle Hill (RIGHT) and Church Lane (BELOW) make clear. Castle Hill is very much the grander, with its wrought-iron railings and symmetrical facades adding distinction to the street. Church Lane, seen here from the churchyard, is less formal; it seems to catch the spirit of the tottering tombstones by the constantly changing lines of the eaves and the shapes of the roofs.

Faversham

KENT

Faversham's life continues, its harbour now handling timber, rather than the exotic produce of the Indies and the Americas. The Guildhall (ABOVE) was built as a market hall in 1574 with an open ground storey supporting an upper hall in the usual way. This was made the Guildhall in 1604. It lasted until 1819 when the hall was rebuilt in a plain classical style, but, since the original octagonal timber posts of the arcade were still serviceable, they were retained.

FAVERSHAM lies at the tip of a creek running into the Swale, the channel that divides Sheppey from the mainland of Kent, and it therefore had direct access to the Thames. So important was this route and the trade it brought that in 1225 the town was ranked with the ancient Cinque Ports, Sandwich, Dover, Hythe, Romney and Hastings.

A century beforehand, King Stephen founded a Cluniac abbey at Faversham. The abbey's wealth was based on farming large estates, of which one was here. The land was rich and the farms produced the wealth to build a large church and other monastic buildings as well as two commodious timber-framed barns. The ruins of the abbey lie beyond the finely conserved houses in Abbey Street, and the abbey's two barns are close by. Faversham's market and port, meanwhile, made it easy for the monks to export their produce.

Times changed. In the 18th century Faversham augmented its legitimate trade in pepper, tea, coffee, calico and tobacco with smuggling, assisted by the Dutch in their oyster boats. This was so lucrative, Defoe recorded, that many people grew 'monstrous rich by that wicked trade'.

Though the date '1570' on No. 10 Market Place (ABOVE) is modern, there is no reason to doubt its veracity as one usually should – most modern dates reflect no more than people's romantic views of the past. This is indeed a fine Elizabethan or early Jacobean timber-framed house, full of the character of its times. The floors and gables typically overhang. They are jettied out by making the floor joists project by a foot or so. This jettying started because it made the assembly of a timber frame easier than it would have been if both the inner and the outer ends of the joists were tenoned into the main framing members. Eventually jettying became a status symbol, showing to the public that a house had an upper storey at a time when

more than one floor was rare. Jetties also had the advantage of making upper rooms larger and of providing shelter to the windows underneath. All that is evident here, and so are the decorative treatment of the framing and the grotesque carving on the brackets that support the sills of the overhanging, oriel windows. Another status symbol is the large area of glass in the front of the house. There was no special need for plenty of light inside the building, but all this glass demonstrated wealth at a time when glazing was both comparatively new and quite expensive.

The view towards Preston Street (RIGHT) is typical of Faversham, with medieval and Tudor houses hiding behind weatherboarding or stylish Georgian facades.

Lewes

EAST SUSSEX

L EWES is the county town of East Sussex. As such, it has a full panoply of civic buildings: a county hall, court, record office, prison and so on. All these were originally housed within the castle, but Lewes's importance goes back further than that. The town was already a defended *burh* (see page 12) by the 9th century, and the line of its High Street, climbing up towards the South Downs from the River Ouse, belongs to that time. The castle was founded after the Norman Conquest by William de Warenne. Unusually it has two mottes, one overlooking the town (*bottom right*), the other overlooking the river as it forces a narrow passage through the Downs to reach the sea a short way down stream at Newhaven.

William de Warenne also founded the Cluniac Priory of St Pancras. It was a great stimulus to Lewes's prosperity, until its French connections became a liability during the Hundred Years' War, and it has been a ruin since the Dissolution of the Monasteries. The railway to Brighton now cuts across its site. The monument of William and his wife was discovered during construction of the line and transferred to Southover church.

The town lies on the hill between the priory and the castle, with little streets and alleys running down from the High Street. Timbering, tiling, brickwork and flint mark its appearance in a happy array of shapes as well as materials.

Although Lewes High Street is full of the town's most notable architecture, there is the constant distraction of side roads leading down from it with precipitous views past old houses out across the estuary of the Ouse. In cobbled Keere Street (RIGHT) the houses are mostly built from flint taken from the South Downs, but, as this makes ragged edges, the doorways and window openings are all lined in brick. In the other direction is the castle (FAR RIGHT).

OVERLEAF: The view from the castle walls is one of the best in Sussex, stretching southwards to the sea at Newhaven, northwards to Ashdown Forest and the Weald. To the left of the view are St Michael's church, which has one of Sussex's three round towers, and the houses facing the High Street, and behind is Southover and the estuary of the Ouse. To the right are the Downs.

This warehouse by the Ouse (RIGHT) and this house in Castle Street seen from the castle Barbican (FAR RIGHT) are both, surprisingly, built of timber. In the warehouse the combination of boarding and tiling makes this fairly obvious, but the house hides behind a remarkable form of tiling that has all the semblance of brickwork. Each tile, which is known as a mathematical tile, is so shaped that the part of it that shows looks exactly like an individual brick and the part that is nailed on to the battens of a timber frame is hidden beneath the exposed parts of the tiles above. The gaps between the tiles are filled with soft mortar or putty, and the deception is complete. With little expense a timber house can be given a stylish Georgian front, complete with a classical porch.

Bowls on the green, being played at Castle Bank (TOP), symbolize the slow pace of English country towns, but an insider would tell a very different story. In the south of England the bowling green is flat, while in the north it rises slightly in the centre and the greens are of different sizes and more rugged in appearance.

The detail ABOVE is from the Town Hall, designed by the architect S. Denman of Brighton and built about 1893 in hard red brick and bright aggressive stucco out of sorts with Lewes's architecture.

Southover High Street (LEFT) may have looked similarly hard when George Harrison built Priory Crescent (on the right-hand side of the picture) in about 1835–45. The brickwork and stuccoing are quite different from the Town Hall's, but they are no more typical of Lewes than of hundreds of other early Victorian towns and suburbs throughout the country. Nevertheless their Georgian style, however mechanically applied, appears on countless other houses in Lewes. The difference can be seen, even so, in the pair of houses on the left, built in the more hand-made fashion that was typical of most houses in country towns until well into the 19th century.

Midhurst

WEST SUSSEX

South Street (ABOVE) looks haphazard, but it was neither purposeless nor contrived to make a pretty view. Each plot had its own builder whose main concern was to do the best for himself within his means. The jettied upper storeys give the houses status and are certainly pretty, but they are also the easiest way to build upper floors.

Midhurst was built on local produce and hard work. The blacksmith (TOP RIGHT) exemplifies a lost world where everything was made by hand.

Mⁱᴅʜᵁᴿˢᵀ is a small market town built in the sheltered fertile vale between the western stretches of the Weald and the wooded scarp of the South Downs. Close by meanders the West Sussex Rother, a tributary of the Arun. On its banks there used to be a castle, and the ruins of the Tudor Cowdray House are in the vicinity.

The town itself, which is all on an enjoyably modest scale, is full of narrow streets that try to make up a kind of irregular grid, but all the time start looping, dividing and rejoining, or simply ramble off, taking a string of cottages with them. All in all, Midhurst is a town of enticing views, a town of timber, tile, brick and stucco.

The church is the one landmark. The Market Place and Old Market House form an undemonstrative centre beside the church, the Market Square and Market Hall another. The triangle at the bottom of Church Hill leads off with a pretty group of cottages and the rather more urban Eagle House and other 18th-century houses in a more purposeful way.

It is easy to assume that so vague a layout is due to chance. In fact each street and each lane once had a purpose. Some led to neighbouring towns, others to fields where people worked or to farms whose produce had to be brought to market.

Sheep Lane loops round from the churchyard to the Market Square. One of its medieval houses (ABOVE) is now the Library, though it lacks the image of municipal purposefulness and academic respectability usually associated with such institutions. In fact, conversion and the accretions of some five centuries have given it the quaint image that is often wrongly associated with the Middle Ages, for medieval houses were not originally as haphazard as this. Its plastered and limewashed panelling contrasts strongly with the herringbone brick nogging used as infilling between the timber members of the framed end of the Spread Eagle (RIGHT), and there is another contrast in the combination of golden Wealden sandstone and local brick used to frame this Georgian window (FAR RIGHT) in South Street.

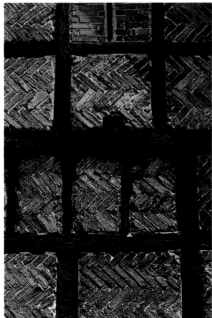

Rye

EAST SUSSEX

The Landgate, seen BELOW *from within the town, was built at the time of the first French raid in 1339, and originally had a portcullis and machicolations. It is the only gate left in the town walls, but not the only evidence of Rye's need for defence. Stretches of wall still lie embedded in the town's buildings where they have overflowed the original town boundaries, and there is Rye's castle, which still survives as the Ypres Tower.*

'RYE would flourish again, if her harbour, which was once able to receive the royal navy could be restored', wrote Daniel Defoe in the 1720s. But the navy changed and the silted-up harbour was left. Even so Rye does flourish again. The yachtsmen who take their boats up the River Rother and the visitors who come to this uncommonly picturesque town keep it alive in a way that the navy never could do.

Rye is built on a sandstone hill overlooking the marshes and shingle of Dungeness. The town's approximate grid of streets, rising and falling over the hill crest, gives shape to the ever-changing, intimate views of timbering, tile-hanging, yellow sandstone and warm red brickwork.

The sea brought trade to Rye, and eventually so much that about 1336 the town attained full status as a Cinque Port. Yet, at the same time, the sea also treated Rye badly. It eroded the sandstone rock on which Rye stands and consumed the eastern parts, and in 1339 it brought French raids. In 1377 the French burnt the town, and there was another raid in 1448.

In the centre of town is the cruciform church, lavishly built in the 12th and 13th centuries and set in a loose square of buildings that includes the 13th-century Flushing Inn. Once a medieval court and market house also stood here, but the present Town Hall, built to the designs of Andrews Jelfe, superseded them about 1743.

Despite the Customs Officers (TOP RIGHT), the Mermaid Inn (TOP CENTRE) was the headquarters of notorious 18th-century smugglers, the Hawkhurst desperadoes. The inn lies at the top of Mermaid Street, which is lined with timber-framed houses down its cobbled path to the tile-hung warehouses on The Quay (TOP LEFT). Lamb House in West Street (ABOVE) was the home of the novelist Henry James from 1898 until his death in 1916. Over the Town Hall cupola, the view from the church tower (RIGHT) stretches to the town walls and beyond.

Sandwich

KENT

Many houses in Sandwich hide behind new fronts added in the 17th and 18th centuries. The Custom House (TOP RIGHT) is one of them. Its modest 18th-century front conceals an interior that goes back at least to the beginning of the 17th century. It is indicative of Sandwich's failure as a port that so modest a building remained adequate for the customs service.

There are several public houses in Sandwich, like the Fleur de Lys (ABOVE), but the coast road only links Thanet with Dover and the town never made enough from the coach trade to replace what it lost as the harbour failed.

Sandwich faces the sheltered but sometimes treacherous bay between the North and South Forelands called the Downs. It was a natural place for a harbour and a sluggish river estuary provided a good mooring.

This is where the Romans landed and built their fort of Rutupiae. A bit further north St Augustine landed on his mission to Canterbury. Here Sandwich grew on exports of wool from the great Benedictine estates of Kent, and so became one of the original Cinque Ports. By the 15th century the river was already silting up, but this coincided with diminishing exports of wool. The harbour exported woollen cloth for a while, and from the 1560s Protestant French and Dutch weavers fleeing religious persecution settled here and gave the town another breath of life, but it was not to last long. Sandwich suffered hard times. In the 1660s the central towers of two of the town's three parish churches collapsed, and money was so tight that the ruins were little more than patched up. Storms washed bars of sand across the river estuary and little by little blocked the harbour. By 1697 Celia Fiennes found Sandwich a 'sad town all timber building', and a generation later Defoe called it 'old, decayed, poor, miserable'. Even today, the town has a stillness that shows how far history has passed it by. Sandwich hardly altered in the 19th century, and has never entirely filled up the space inside its town walls.

In many ways Sandwich remains a medieval town, complete with its town ditch and walls, a main gate called the Barbican, the Cattle Market and Guildhall, and Strand Street full of medieval houses. The coast road enters Sandwich from the north by way of a toll bridge over the River Stour. Here the town is protected by the Barbican (ABOVE). The bulging form of its 16th-century bastion is emphasized by chequered decoration in stone and flint.

St Mary's (RIGHT) is one of the two churches whose towers fell in the 1660s. Beyond are several 16th-century timber-framed houses including one of many in the town with a continuous upper storey jettied out at the front.

Sandwich has plenty of room inside its walls for houses with extensive gardens, such as the one belonging to the house in Moatside on the LEFT. *The garden front of this house is of no great age and probably goes back only to the early 19th century, but this house by St Peter's (*ABOVE*), though heavily rebuilt in the 18th or 19th century, has flint walls that are almost certainly medieval. The church tower in the background is the other of the two that fell in the 1660s, and was repaired only in the 18th century.*

Tunbridge Wells

KENT

The first visitors to the Wells were Royalists, and, to counter local puritanism, the new church of 1676–80 was dedicated to St Charles the Martyr (OPPOSITE AND ABOVE, LEFT). Outside it is plain, except for the charming clock turret, but its real glory is the plaster ceiling, executed by John Wetherel and Henry Dogood.

No pedestrian precinct is better than the Pantiles (RIGHT AND ABOVE, RIGHT). It was laid out in 1638, and rebuilt in 1687 with a colonnade. The formal Tuscan columns and informal pollarded lime trees of its curving path, and the weatherboarding jostling with tile-hanging and stucco with bright red bricks would be counted genius if they were the work of any one controlling mind. Celia Fiennes came to the Pantiles in 1697 to take the water. She saw 'high trees on the market side for shade and secured with a row of buildings on the right side which are shopps full of all sorts of toys, silver, china, milliners . . . besides which there are two large Coffee houses for Tea Chocolate etc.'

TUNBRIDGE WELLS is a new town. Approaching from the north, you first come to Southborough, which sounds all wrong until you realize that it is the south borough of the town of Tonbridge. Beyond it once lay the densely packed oaks of the Weald, and heavy impassable tracts of water-logged clay. The courtier Dudley, Lord North, was returning to London and the high life when he noticed a spring of water here because of the 'shining mineral scum that everywhere swam on its surface . . .'

This was caused by the iron ore that had given the Weald its most famous industry, but out of such trivial beginnings a town was made. North made his discovery in 1606 – some say 1615 or 1616 – and soon the beneficial effects of the springs had attracted no less than Queen Henrietta Maria. By the 1720s, as Defoe recorded, 'The ladies that appear here, are indeed the glory of the place; the coming to the Wells to drink the water is a mere matter of custom . . . company and diversion is in short the main business of the place . . .' So Tunbridge Wells grew up, a town in the midst of woods, as it still is, 'without plan or semblance of regularity', and an ideal setting for 'rural romatic retirement'.

Windsor

BERKSHIRE

Lying in the shadow of Fitch's Town Hall is the old Market Cross House (BELOW) and, behind that, the Shambles, a name that has picturesque associations, but was a place traditionally reserved for abattoirs and butchers. The past was not so inherently picturesque as some people believe, but every age tends to see the past in these terms. This is how George IV saw his medieval castle, though it was not sufficiently picturesque for his taste and so he had it reworked.

No castle in England is more extensive than Windsor's, no town more completely dominated by its castle.

The castle owes its strength to a strategically placed island of chalk forming a steep cliff overlooking a curve of the River Thames. A handsome park for hunting added to its attractions, and the river provided a quick route to the capital. William the Conqueror saw these advantages and began building. Practically every king and queen has added to the castle, but its romantic image today is the result of two major works. The first is Edward IV's St George's Chapel, a prodigious building worthy of kings and the ancient Order of the Garter whose chapel it also is. Then, superimposed on the castle, there are the additions and enlargements of George IV's architect, Sir Jeffry Wyatville, in 1820–30. He raised the Round Tower (*opposite*) by 33 feet to make it the building's dominating feature and added battlements and towers.

Though the town is an appendage of the castle, it is not entirely subdued by it. First among its buildings is the Town Hall (see page 11), designed by an architect practically no one knows, Sir Thomas Fitch, and finished after his death in 1689 by an architect every one knows, Sir Christopher Wren. He, incidentally, lived in Windsor for a year or two as an infant when his father was Dean of Windsor.

Images of Windsor: the old Great Western Railway terminus (TOP LEFT), the late 12th-century keep with Wyatville's machicolations and parapet (TOP RIGHT), and a Georgian corner in Park Street (ABOVE). Nell Gwyn's house (LEFT) is curiously narrow; it would be nice to think of her sticky, orange-scented fingers opening its front door to a royal visitor, but the truth is that if she had occupied every house accredited to her, she would never have had any time for Charles II.

The West Country

DEVON
DORSET · SOMERSET
WILTSHIRE

THE West Country is even more diverse in character than the south-east. It has never been united by the wealth that London brought to the Home Counties, and all that can be generally said about it is that its winters are mild, its summers are wet and the moors that cover much of the further parts are notably bleak and poor.

The Romans, therefore, were not greatly interested in the west beyond Exeter: the wealth of Somerset and Dorset with their good arable and pasture land was what counted. Towns like Dorchester became important administrative and economic centres, and did so again after a fresh start in the centuries that followed the departure of Rome. Some of Wiltshire, though, was a backwater, and Salisbury Plain hardly better than Dartmoor, but local sheep and plentiful water supplies made towns like Salisbury, Malmesbury and Bradford-on-Avon important centres for weaving at a time when most wool was exported to be woven abroad.

When weaving was taken up on a large scale in the second half of the 14th century, many towns with a decent water supply followed their lead. This gave Tiverton its chance and indeed many other towns in the western half of the country grew fat on the cloth trade, while others such as Totnes (*left*) developed the harbours through which the cloth was exported.

The West Country is marked apart from the south-east by its plentiful building stone. The hard granite of Dartmoor was taken off the ground and used for modest buildings as early as the 14th century when elsewhere they were still made of cob, a mixture of mud, pebbles and straw. Three centuries later all the region's stones were in use, and a very varied lot they are, both in colour and quality. They include soft red sandstones, harder yellow sandstones, blue Lias and honey-hued oölite. Then there is the best of all, the fine white Portland stone of Dorset that was exported as far as London and even America so great was the demand for it.

Barnstaple

DEVON

*After the Dissolution of the Monasteries,
numerous charities took over the care of the
aged and built almshouses. These were
groups of small homes with one or two rooms,
as exemplified by the Horwood Almshouses in
Church Lane (BELOW), which have two blocks
of houses, built in 1659 and 1674. The
inmates were often carefully selected, for
instance by membership of the trade or guild
that founded the almshouses. Apart from free
accommodation, they also received a small
pension and certain gifts, such as items of
food.*

Barnstaple is the most important commercial town in north Devon. It owes this to its situation at the head of the Taw estuary, an ideal place for a sheltered port. The water here was neither too wide nor too deep for a bridge, and the much-widened medieval bridge still spans the water on sixteen arches (see page 27). From here a trade route led inland along the river to cross the county, eventually to reach Tiverton, Exeter and the south coast.

The town was made a borough in 930, and was allowed to mint its own coins. Wool was the major export until the 17th century, but as this trade declined others arose. The port served the American colonies, and dealt in wine. Wool was soon imported rather than exported, and came from Ireland to be sent down to Tiverton and Exeter. Trade was augmented by a herring fishery, second in the amount of fish it cured only to Bideford's. This together with shipping and ship-building kept the town going until the 1880s when other ports took the trade and the river silted up.

By then Barnstaple was a town of Georgian shops and houses, lining a series of pretty lanes running off the High Street. Many of the most imposing buildings owe their existence to the thriving foreign trade.

Opposite Barnstaple Bridge is The Square with The Golden Lion Tap facing it (LEFT). This old coaching inn claims a 16th-century origin. This may come from the date of a licence, but the licence may not be the inn's first. So the origin of the inn could be earlier still. None the less the buildings themselves have probably been rebuilt so many times that they have little resemblance to their originals. The front looks as though it belongs to the early 19th century, and the rest seems to be of all kinds of dates.

Until refrigeration became available at the end of the 19th century, the fish landed at Barnstaple were salted or smoked if they were to travel. Nowadays most old fishing ports have more on sale than the local catch. So it is likely that most of the fish in the shop LEFT was caught far away, leaving the herrings landed at Barnstaple as a local speciality.

Pottery (ABOVE) again can maintain its local traditions even though much of the craft is subject to processes as modern as those that have changed fishmongering.

Blandford Forum

DORSET

Beside the church in the centre of Blandford Forum there is a monument erected in 1760 to contain a water-pump and the inscription 'In grateful Acknowledgement of the DIVINE MERCY, that has raised this Town, like the PHAENIX from it's ashes, to it's present beautiful and flourishing State.'

The inscription recalls the devastating fire of 1731, which indeed burnt the town to ashes. Luckily two builders of vision were at hand. John and William Bastard were civic dignitaries of Blandford as well as master builders, surveyors and architects, so their qualifications matched their opportunity.

Over the next thirty years they rebuilt the town, widening the Market Place a little, but otherwise leaving the street pattern alone. They designed and built a new church and Town Hall, and saw to the rebuilding of much of the rest of Blandford. Their taste for the baroque style displayed in these buildings was a bit old fashioned for the 1730s, but the result is one of the happiest Georgian towns in the country, the stone civic buildings blending with the varied hues of the local bricks into a composition at once friendly and dignified.

Blandford church was rebuilt by the Bastards in 1733–9. The tower is placed at the west end, and, from the distance (OPPOSITE, BELOW), has a medieval outline. The church's baroque details show clearly in the lower part of the tower (RIGHT), where the entrance and the window to the upper chamber form a linked composition. The details come from illustrations of the work of 17th-century Italian architects, but, instead of the intensity and religious fervour of the Italian baroque style, they have the coolness and even rationality so prevalent in 18th-century England. The overall harmony and balance that they give to the church is classical. The round arch of the entrance, for instance, is balanced by the round pediment over the upper window, and the straight head of the cornice over the entrance is balanced once again by the straight head of the window lintel. These small but seemingly effortless points of design harmonize all the parts of the west front into a splendidly unified composition.

East Street (RIGHT) and West Street (BELOW) show the remarkably homogeneous architecture of Blandford Forum. The regular facades are relieved by the gentle curve of the streets and the occasional accent of a lower house with dormers to light its garrets. The sash windows are subtly varied either in size or by curved or straight arches over them, and some have stucco keystones. So, by ringing the changes with a few details, the whole scene comes to life. This hardly detracts from the twin focuses of the church tower and the porticoed front of the Town Hall.

Bradford-on-Avon

WILTSHIRE

The medieval bridge at Bradford-on-Avon (BELOW) was largely rebuilt in the 17th century. The little chapel for travellers was also rebuilt and became the Blind House, that is to say a lockup.

The roof of the Barton Farm barn (OPPOSITE) has the most ornate timberwork of any barn in the country. Great curving timbers called crucks rise up in two tiers to span the roof, and there are large numbers of curved bracing timbers to support the purlins and rafters on each side.

By far the oldest building in Bradford-on-Avon is the church of St Lawrence. It lay unrecognized until about 1857 when the vicar, looking across the roofs piled up on the steeply embanked slope on which the town is built, spotted a cross he had not seen before. This belonged to a small monastic church that was founded about 700 and perhaps largely rebuilt early in the 11th century when the monastery belonged to the Benedictine nuns of Shaftesbury Abbey.

The Church continued its influence in this beautiful small town, notably in the 14th century when the nuns built one of the finest of all medieval barns at Barton Farm on the south side of the river. In doing so, they vested agriculture with the semblance of Ceres, and gave to an everyday type of building the monumentality of a temple.

Weaving brought no temples, but many of the town's houses came from the profits of this industry. 'They told me at Bradford', Daniel Defoe wrote, 'that it was no extraordinary thing to have clothiers [i.e. manufacturers of cloth] in the country worth from ten thousand, to forty thousand pounds a man, and many of the great families, who now pass for gentry . . . have originally been raised from, and built up by this truly noble manufacture.' This wealth continued into the 18th century, when the first factories were built down by the river.

The date of the Anglo-Saxon church is a puzzle that adds poignancy to its fine but simple detailing (LEFT). About 1120 the historian William of Malmesbury stated that Aldhelm, Abbot of Bradford, had built a little church 'in the name of the Most Blessed Lawrence', apparently for the monastery the abbot had founded before he became Bishop of Sherborne in 705. There is little doubt that this was the present church, but it is hard to know how much of the surviving fabric belongs to this early date. It is likely that most of what can be seen was built soon after King Ethelred II granted the manor of Bradford and its monastery to the nuns of Shaftesbury Abbey in 1001. In any case, it is one of the most remarkable Saxon churches in England.

Early in the 16th century Bradford's wealth from weaving was already evident in its earliest stone houses. There was the rich clothier Thomas Horton who built the Old Church House, and whose monument is in the parish church. Then there is The Hall, built about 1610 not as a manorial hall, but as a demonstration of the profits a certain John Hall made from the cloth industry. Lesser men lived in lesser houses, such as this row of 17th-century cottages climbing up the side of Coppice Hill. They are in their way more typical of the wealth weaving brought to the town than the more occasional grand houses. Yet even these cottages are made from some of the finest building stone in the country.

However lavish and church-like in construction, Barton Farm's medieval barn (ABOVE) was built for the storage of corn and the threshing and winnowing of grain. It was a house of toil, for threshing and winnowing were back-breaking tasks. Its idyllic setting is today's interpretation of the view, and was probably not shared by the men who worked there. The same is true of this view of the Kennett and Avon Canal (RIGHT), laid out by the engineer John Rennie and opened in 1810 as an important trunk route for heavy goods between Bristol and Bath, and Reading and London.

Dorchester

DORSET

Prison reforms by John Howard in the late 18th century led to purpose-built prisons replacing castle jails in many county towns. Dorchester was no exception, even in maintaining a link with the old castle site. Most of the present red-brick prison buildings (ABOVE) were erected in 1884–5, but beyond them is the portal of the first prison built in Portland stone by Howard's friend the reformer William Blackburn in 1790–2.

HERE, in the heart of Thomas Hardy's Wessex, civilization can be traced back deep into prehistory. Mount Pleasant to the east and then Maiden Castle to the south-west were important settlements until the Roman legions overcame Maiden Castle's defences in AD 43 or 44 and sacked it.

That gave Dorchester its start as the Roman town of Durnovaria, capital of the tribe of Durotriges. Little has been excavated. Nevertheless the town's importance as the junction of roads leading north, south, east and west and as a crossing over the River Frome has not changed, and Dorchester is now the county town of Dorset.

The Norman castle has largely vanished, but one of its functions is still accommodated on the same site in the red brick prison. As a centre of justice, Dorchester is notorious for Judge Jeffreys's 'bloody assize', held after the Monmouth rebellion in 1685, and also for the trial of the Tolpuddle Martyrs in the Old Shire Hall in 1834.

The Shire Hall is a dignified classical building of Portland Stone, the finest stone in the country and entirely appropriate for the county's headquarters, though much of the rest of the town is built of cheaper brick made from local clay. The centre of Dorchester was swept by many fires in the 18th century, but they were not as devastating as the fire at Blandford Forum. Rebuilding was piecemeal and full of variety. This inspired Hardy's Casterbridge, whose future mayor Henchard sold his wife at a local fair.

Hangman's Cottage (ABOVE) is typical of many of Dorset's small houses, with low walls, dormer windows peeping from beneath a heavy thatched roof and warm, red brick walls that probably replaced ones built originally of cob, a mixture of mud, pebbles and straw. But, like so much in this pleasant town of welcoming views, there lurks over it the more sinister qualities of a long history of violence that started with the massacre at Maiden Castle, the hanging and quartering of seventy-four men convicted by Judge Jeffreys and the scattering of their bloody remains around the county, and the misery of the Tolpuddle Martyrs. Over all, there is the morbid, brooding presence of Thomas Hardy, who darkened the whole Dorset scenery with his pessimistic view of frail values collapsing before the onrush of his own times.

Opposite the parish church in the centre of Dorchester is the King's Arms Hotel (RIGHT). Its generously proportioned front dates from the early 19th century, and gives the street a landmark befitting the hotel's purpose. As much an inn sign as the one hanging outside is the centrepiece of the hotel front, an open porch on Tuscan columns supporting a great semicircular bay with five sash windows on both storeys filling most of it. Here at least everything seems to be sweetness and light.

Glastonbury

SOMERSET

Glastonbury Tor (ABOVE) is a 500-foot hump of Triassic stone, left behind after eroding seas levelled the land all around to form the Somerset Levels and drowned them in peaty alluvium. Today it broods over the town, as it must have brooded over the Iron Age settlements long before the lone medieval tower was raised on its crest. It is an outstanding landmark, and so curiously sited, terraced and shaped that it is hardly surprising how much it has added romance to the town at its foot.

'THE venerable marks of antiquity', wrote Defoe about Glastonbury, 'struck me with some unusual awe'. Here was Avalon where King Arthur was buried. Here Joseph of Arimathea brought the Holy Grail, and founded the abbey.

Glastonbury is still full of awe. It was just outside the town that the Lake Villages were founded, and their excavation opened up a vivid impression of Iron Age communities living two thousand years ago. At the foot of Glastonbury Tor lie the abbey and the grid of streets forming the old town. Here also marks of antiquity abound. The abbey is truly ancient. It was founded – or at least refounded – by King Ine about 700, and here St Dunstan was a monk and then abbot. King Edgar's body was laid here in 975, and many of the buildings of those days are known, thanks again to archaeological excavation.

If the abbey once dominated the town, the town is nevertheless no mere appendage, even though it is dotted with the abbey's buildings such as the spectacular George Hotel and the Tribunal. Its business was wool, and this and rich local agriculture have made it thrive and continue to thrive long after the abbey was divested of its power and wealth.

The George Hotel (LEFT) in the High Street was once an inn where pilgrims to the abbey could stay. All abbeys had a guest house, many built inns, but here is an inn way beyond the normal. It is not just a rare survivor, but also extremely sumptuous in its decoration and in its arrangements. It has three storeys, with the middle one treated as the main floor for public rooms. The exterior is covered in a grid of panelling that embraces the windows and the archway which gives access to a rear courtyard. Over the arch are the arms of the abbey and Edward IV, suggesting that The George was built in the 1470s or 80s.

The more extensive abbey buildings that superseded those in which King Edgar was buried were put up in phases in the 12th, 13th and 14th centuries. Much is still visible despite ruination, especially the east side of the crossing and transepts (ABOVE), which were begun in 1184. The intact Monks' Kitchen and the abbey barn, outside the precinct, also survive, and it is still possible to see the site south of the Lady Chapel where in 1191 the monks found what they claimed to be the burial place of King Arthur and Queen Guinevere. The tomb was placed before the high altar, where the antiquary Leland saw it in the 1530s.

Malmesbury

WILTSHIRE

The banks of the Avon (BELOW) are lined by a number of fine mills. Water was indispensable for weaving and could also power some of the implements used in the manufacture of cloth. So to the river's defensive role was added an economic role. By the 18th century, when the weaving of woollen textiles was declining before the greater efficiency of other places, the town turned to silk, and it was the weaving of this luxury that caused the mills in the background to be built.

MALMESBURY lies above the Bristol Avon on a low hill of Cornbrash limestone rising above the Oxford clay of the valleys, and just south-east of the Fosse Way. This was the great Roman road that runs to this day, straight and bare, across the country, dividing the rich south-eastern half of England from the poorer north-west. It was a strategic site, so Malmesbury became one of King Alfred's *burhs* (see page 12) and stood in the front line of Saxon defences against the Danes.

Malmesbury's tangible beginnings lie in its abbey, founded in the 7th century, and burnt and built again twice before the present building was started in the 12th century and given some of the finest medieval carving in the country. Luckily it was not entirely ruined again at the Dissolution. The nave was purchased by a prosperous clothier William Stumpe, and given to the town as its parish church.

As an Anglo-Saxon *burh*, Malmesbury soon had a flourishing market. Like several other Wiltshire towns, it was one of the earliest centres of weaving to be established in the country and this brought the wealth that eventually raised the abbey tower higher than Salisbury's. But the tower fell, and it is in the fine houses and inns that the town's former prosperity can be judged now.

The Market Cross (BELOW) was built about 1500, 'for poore folkes to stande dry when rayne commeth', recorded John Leland, the great Tudor antiquary. It is one of the finest medieval crosses in the country, and compares with the better-known ones in Salisbury and Chichester. The ribs of its vaulted interior rise, appropriately almost like an umbrella, from the central pier to make flat Tudor arches that are reflected in the eight, flat-arched openings round its perimeter. The whole structure seems purposeful and logical, although it was built as a status symbol as much as for utility, and designed to show off Malmesbury's role as a successful commercial centre. The three-legged dog RIGHT belongs to the pub next door to the Tolsey Gate.

Many of Malmesbury's houses back on to the River Avon (LEFT), as seen here with the spire of St Paul's church rising above them.

The picturesque attraction of this view is worlds apart from the conscious artistry of the south porch of the Abbey Church, built about 1160–70 in the last great flowering of the Norman style. It has a finely carved entrance arch and two semi-circular panels inside, each of which depicts six of the twelve apostles with an angel flying overhead (ABOVE). The figures all adopt expressive yet stylized positions, and the folds of their robes are treated as an opportunity for the carver to indulge in abstract pattern-making as the cloth rises and falls over the apostles' knees. This style had appeared in the great west front of Lincoln Cathedral some twenty years beforehand, but its origin is French, or, rather, Burgundian. It was often used in Burgundy earlier in the 12th century and nowhere more marvellously than at Autun about 1130. Craftsmen travelled widely around Europe in the Middle Ages, and, although the origin of the carving at Malmesbury is quite unknown, there is no reason at all why Burgundians should not have been at work here.

From the 17th century onwards tombstones show the ordinary lives and deaths of people rich enough to be commemorated in stone (RIGHT). Poor Hannah Twynnoy's death was, however, far from ordinary.

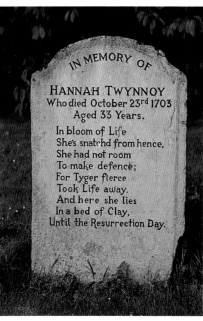

IN MEMORY OF

HANNAH TWYNNOY
Who died October 23rd 1703
Aged 33 Years.

In bloom of Life
She's snatchd from hence,
She had not room
To make defence;
For Tyger fierce
Took Life away,
And here she lies
In a bed of Clay,
Until the Resurrection Day.

Marlborough

WILTSHIRE

Charles Sorley, the World War I poet, who was a pupil at the College, called Marlborough 'our old wrinkled red-capped town'. After the fires, timber and thatch were outlawed, making a town of warm brick and red tiles. The new rules were not stringently applied, and timber frames with tile-hung or brick fronts passed muster. The High Street and Kingsbury Street (BELOW) are consequently very wrinkled and show the joins between the different building materials used on the individual houses and shops.

MARLBOROUGH boasts the widest market street in England. It is also spectacularly long and subtly curved, gracefully following the line of the River Kennett, which runs a short way below it. With a church tucked away at each end, Marlborough College just beyond to the west, and the Town Hall to the east, it all seems to be of great antiquity.

Appearances are deceptive in this town, whose ancient remains are mere fragments. The reason lies in Marlborough's violent past. Once there were a royal castle, a Gilbertine priory and a house of Carmelite friars, but the Civil War brought fierce fighting, and then in 1653 fire swept the town. The first attempts at rebuilding were frustrated by fire a second time in 1679, and again in 1690.

So most of the buildings of any substance came after the late 17th century. The College occupies one impressive house of this period, C-House, an outstanding example of Queen Anne architecture. But the College was founded only in 1843, and its first school buildings are in the same style, sensitively revived to match. Later, almost inevitably in so earnest a century, further College buildings were put up in a revived Gothic. This style, so the Victorians thought, was the epitome of medieval morality, and what could be better for schoolboys than that?

At one end of the High Street is The Parade (FAR RIGHT), where an arcade shelters the shop fronts and supports the decorative tiling and bay windows of the floors above. There is more decorative tiling around St Mary's churchyard (BELOW). Here and there are formal touches like the porch in Kingsbury Street (RIGHT), which is elegantly Grecian and belongs to the later 18th century, when this sort of classicism was like a stylish set of clothes.

Shaftesbury

DORSET

Just off the High Street, surprisingly unmarked and reached almost unawares, is one of the best-loved views in the country. Here town suddenly meets country, strongly evoking the past. Cobbled Gold Hill, modest stone cottages to one side, buttressed abbey walls to the other, curves down towards far-off Blackmoor in a breathtaking sweep.

SHAFTESBURY lies on a commanding spur of Greensand overlooking the broad Vale of Blackmoor to the south-west. This made it a fitting site for defence. So King Alfred founded one of his *burhs* here and fortified it against the Danes. He especially favoured Shaftesbury, and fostered it in about 880 with the gift of his own daughter Ethelgiva to be the first abbess of a Benedictine abbey of nuns.

The abbey's nuns became the richest in England, counting the great barn at Bradford-on-Avon among their possessions. The town flourished too, and did well out of the cloth trade in the later Middle Ages. At one time it boasted four market crosses as well as twelve churches and a castle, not to mention all the lesser buildings that served the burgesses.

The Dissolution destroyed the abbey, and the castle has left no trace but a bare patch at the west end of the hilltop. Many buildings were demolished, especially in the 18th century. Despite its cloth industry, Daniel Defoe found Shaftesbury 'a sorry town' in the 1720s, and, a century and a half later, Thomas Hardy viewed it, 'all now ruthlessly swept away', with pensive melancholy.

Nevertheless the High Street still takes its angled course along the hill crest, and fragments of former wealth show in patches. At least the site remains and, from it, the magnificent views across the Dorset countryside.

In 1820 the Earl of Grosvenor bought large parts of Shaftesbury to control the voting in what was then a rotten borough. Four years later came the Grosvenor Hotel and in it is the luxurious carving of the 'Chevy Chase' sideboard (LEFT), carved 1857–63 by Gerrard Robinson of Newcastle.

In the suburb of St James below the town is this delightful quadrangle of houses forming Old Pump Court (LEFT). A thatched dormer (TOP), typical of Dorset, has an owl decorating its crest. Severely plain walls (ABOVE) give way to large curved windows at the corner of this street.

Sherborne

DORSET

During the 15th century the Abbey Church (ABOVE LEFT) was rebuilt in a glorious Perpendicular style. In the choir the fine fan-vault was raised about 1450 to become the earliest major one in the country. All this work was executed in golden Ham Hill stone, brought from just across the county boundary. It contributes in no small way to the overwhelmingly rich impression given by the church and its neighbouring buildings, which include the medieval almshouses of St John the Baptist (ABOVE, RIGHT).

Some of the abbey buildings have gone, others are now incorporated into Sherborne School, but just to the east of the church is a tiny square with a conduit (ABOVE, CENTRE) in the middle. It was built by Abbot Mere at the start of the 16th century as the monks' lavatorium or washplace; after the Dissolution it was removed and made into the Market Cross.

Unlike the abbey, the old castle was detached from the town, as this view from it (RIGHT) shows. It was started by Bishop Roger of Salisbury between 1107 and 1135 and lasted until its demolition by Parliament after the Civil War.

THE Romans favoured the warm valley at the head of the River Yeo that now shelters Sherborne, and so did the Saxons. In 705 the growing town was already important enough for King Ine to divide the diocese of Winchester and make Sherborne the see of the Bishop of Wessex. The church became a cathedral until 1075, when the see was transferred to Old Sarum (later superseded by Salisbury). By then the abbey had been founded, and it took the old Saxon church, and incorporated it into its precinct.

At the Dissolution of the Monasteries in 1539, the now rebuilt church survived to serve the parish, and out of the abbey school came the present public school, founded by Edward VI and transformed between 1850 and 1877 by its headmaster, the Reverend H.B. Harper. Despite the changes, abbey, school and almshouses, built in 1437–8 for twelve poor men and four poor women, present a golden image of medieval piety, learning and charity.

None of these could support a town like Sherborne by itself, but dairy farming brought wealth to this part of Dorset in the 16th and 17th centuries and Sherborne developed an important market. Farming still supports the town, and a factory for dairy products continues the tradition. So unlike Shaftesbury, Sherborne continued to flourish. Silk weaving came in the 1740s, and soon a factory was built for it, part of which survives, though silk weaving has been replaced by the manufacture of fibreglass.

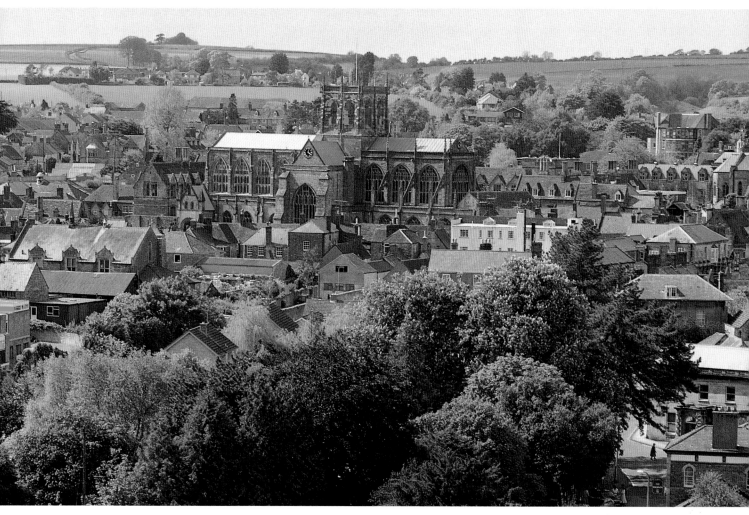

From the hills to the south (ABOVE), the abbey appears to dominate the town, though in fact it lies towards the bottom of the slope on which the town is built and very much at Sherborne's southern edge. Nevertheless its great, buttressed walls pierced by expansive windows filled with tracery stand up proudly over the roofs.

Clustering round the other side of the church are the buildings of the school, many of them started by Harper in the 1850s, 60s and 70s, some incorporating parts of the former abbey buildings. The original schoolroom was built in 1606–8.

Hidden by the trees in the foreground is the railway, which kept Sherborne from stagnating in the 19th century. It lay on the London and South Western Railway's main line to Exeter and carried the famous Atlantic Coast Express, but is perhaps lucky to survive today as a single-track branch line.

The old castle at Sherborne was a comfortable, palatial building and not particularly well suited to defence. It was nevertheless held for Charles I in the Civil War and this caused it to be destroyed afterwards. Well before that, though, it had been superseded by a second castle. This owes its origin to Sir Walter Raleigh. He leased the old castle in 1592, but soon started the new one a quarter of a mile away (RIGHT). This was to be a grand country house with a simple rectangular plan and polygonal turrets. After Raleigh's downfall, the house was enlarged by the Digbys who took over the estate, and its bizarre outline is the result, even though they kept to Raleigh's style. The new castle gains much from Capability Brown's landscaping. He remodelled the park in 1756 and 1776–9, and dammed the stream to form a lake that sets off both the new castle and the ruins of the old.

Tavistock

DEVON

The railway through Tavistock was part of a branch line jointly owned by the Great Western Railway and the London and South Western Railway that ran from Plymouth and Devonport around the west and north of Dartmoor to join the LSWR line from Exeter to Barnstaple. Its meandering course did not help its purpose and it was closed in the 1960s. Nevertheless, the imposing railway viaduct at Tavistock (BELOW) still strides across the road that runs westwards out of town.

TAVISTOCK takes its name from the River Tavy, and lies where the river flows down from the south-west flank of Dartmoor. Here in 981 the Benedictines founded what became their wealthiest and most powerful abbey in Devon, and the town grew up in its shadow. The early wealth of the abbey came from agricultural products, especially wool, but by the 13th century this was augmented by tin, and in 1305 Taunton became one of Devon's four 'stannary' towns, named after its stannary court, which regulated the manufacture and sale of the metal. But tin production declined in about 1500, leaving Tavistock's prosperity to expand over the next two hundred years with the cloth trade. Meanwhile a parish church was built hard against the abbey walls and dedicated in 1318. With so much money in the town, it was soon largely rebuilt and enlarged with the Clothworkers' Aisle, financed from donations made in 1445.

In 1539 the abbey was dissolved and granted to Sir John Russell as a reward for his services to the Crown. He continued to serve and later became Lord Privy Seal. For all this he was created first Earl of Bedford. Politics paid in Tudor times, provided you kept your head. He kept his, and so Tavistock's future was bound up with the fortunes of the family thereafter. The abbey was pulled down, but both Tavistock and the Russells did well, especially the Russells.

Early in the 19th century, the Russells, now Dukes of Bedford, promoted mining on the moors above the town, mainly for lead, silver, zinc and copper. The ore was brought down to the town by a new canal (BELOW) which followed the river from Mary Tavy. This brought great wealth to the Russells and gave them an opportunity to modernize the town with new buildings in the sombre local gritstone.

With the abbey gone, the parish church now lies by itself surrounded by the tombstones of Tavistock's worthy citizens (RIGHT). Nearby is the centre of the town with a bridge of 1773 over the Tavy leading into it. On part of the abbey's grounds is the Bedford Hotel, built early in the 18th century but Gothicized about 1820. There are several civic buildings erected by the Russells in various medieval styles here, and, to the south of the town, the cottages (BELOW) which they built for their copper miners.

Tiverton

DEVON

In 1731 the centre of Tiverton was devastated by fire. Rebuilding began immediately afterwards using the old street pattern. In St Andrew's Street (BELOW) is St George's church, built as a large auditorium of local red sandstone and embellished with a classical pediment over the west front and a cupola above. The extraordinarily elaborate Town Hall opposite of 1864 was designed by a Bristol architect, Henry Lloyd, in a hotchpotch of baroque styles with more than a dash of French dressing around the roof.

TIVERTON's original name Twyford means between two rivers, the Exe and its tributary the Lowman. Its strategic site was exploited by the Anglo-Saxons when they reached this far west in the 7th century. Then in 1106 Richard de Redvers, first Earl of Devon, founded a castle on the steep bluff overlooking the Exe valley. Tiverton's later prosperity still relied on the river. It provided an important trade route both along its valley northwards into the heart of Devon to Barnstaple, and southwards down its navigable waters to Exeter. Furthermore the river's fresh, clear water made it possible to weave local wool into fine kersey. Appropriately, therefore, it was a rich wool merchant, Peter West, who built himself a house about 1700 within the walls of the now ruined castle.

Unlike many weaving towns in the West Country, Tiverton's prosperity continued in the 19th century. Paradoxically the town can thank the Luddite riots for that. Just as the old weaving industry was declining, rioters destroyed John Heathcote's lace-making factory at Loughborough in Leicestershire, and he received £10,000 compensation. With it he brought his machines to Tiverton and set them up in a factory on the further side of the river. This burnt down and was replaced in 1936, but by then the suburb of West Exe had grown up in front of it with a church and a dignified group of spacious streets. Now the firm makes all kinds of products from synthetics to farm machinery.

Civic pride has given Tiverton much attractive housing, including a quadrangle (ABOVE), a pretty alternative to the wide streets of West Exe.

St Peter's church is a more prominent monument of ancient civic pride. Consecrated soon after the Norman Conquest, it was rebuilt with an ostentatious tower about 1400, and then rebuilt again and extended in the 16th and 17th centuries when wealthy merchants poured money into the work. John Greenway paid for the sumptuous chantry chapel and porch of 1517. The chapel has a frieze of ships and the arms of the Merchant Venturers' and Drapers' Companies. The porch is carved with eagles, fish and other motifs (RIGHT). Inside there is a carving of the Assumption of the Virgin flanked by the kneeling donor and his wife and, lest there be any mistake, his initials.

Totnes

DEVON

The approach to castle and church is up the steep Fore Street to the town walls, now represented by North Street and South Street, through the East Gate (OPPOSITE), and on up High Street. Beyond Butterwalk the street narrows before the entry to the castle (BELOW). This has the classic pattern of Norman castles, with a steeply built-up motte set within an embanked bailey. The original square, timber tower was soon replaced by a stone circular keep and outer walls.

TOTNES lies at the head of the tortuous Dart estuary, on a commanding spur with a castle to guard a port and river crossing.

Legend would have Totnes founded in 1170 BC by Brutus the Trojan. More credibly it was founded as a Saxon royal *burh*, and was already minting its own coins and successfully trading through the port in the 10th century. At that stage, earthen ramparts defended the town and these were later strengthened in stone.

After William had conquered Devon in 1068, he gave Totnes to the Breton adventurer Judhael de Totenais, who, it is said, built the castle. Judhael also gave a church to Totnes Priory, but the parish church erected beside the priory in the middle of the 15th century in seductive red Devonian sandstone was a different foundation, built in competition with the priory.

The many fine houses in Totnes owe their existence to the wealth brought through the port in the 16th and 17th centuries, with tin and cloth going to France, canvas and linen coming back. Further up the hill, past the church and the modest Guildhall, the High Street widens to form a vestigial square before branching to left and right in front of the castle hill. Here are the pretty arcaded houses of the Butterwalk, set over columns of timber, iron and stone. Many of the houses are faced in slate to keep off the rain that drives across the open square.

At the bottom of Fore Street is The Plain and the River Dart, still lined with warehouses (ABOVE), evidence of flourishing trade continuing right up to the 20th century.

No. 70 Fore Street, now a museum, graphically shows the typical arrangements of Totnes houses in the 16th and 17th centuries. It is timber framed and set between stone party walls, with the front jettied and gabled. A passageway leads to a yard at the back where a separate kitchen block is linked to the house by a gallery. The jetties are supported by brackets carved with grotesque heads (FAR LEFT), and others adorn the keystones of later houses (LEFT). The castle set the tone for several buildings in Totnes, notably the East Gate and the Gothic house (RIGHT) in Back Lane off Fore Street.

The Heart of England

GLOUCESTERSHIRE · HEREFORD AND WORCESTER · OXFORDSHIRE SHROPSHIRE · WARWICKSHIRE

THE west Midlands were formerly poorer than the east Midlands. Edward I's conquest of Wales at the end of the 13th century changed that and brought peace and eventual prosperity to a region blessed with a mild climate and a great variety of soils to benefit from it. The worst soils were on the Cotswolds, but local sheep and rushing streams in narrow valleys fostered the cloth industry, and many towns grew fat on the profits. Chipping Campden is the most famous on account of its wide High Street and sumptuous 'wool' church built from the fine honey-coloured Jurassic limestone of the Cotswolds, but it is by no means alone. Ludlow not only did well out of wool, but also flourished as the provincial capital from which Wales was ruled, where previously it had suffered from its unruly neighbour.

The vales of the west Midlands were good for cattle, fruit, and specialized crops like hops. Ledbury benefited from all these, particularly the famous Herefordshire cattle. Ross-on-Wye was a centre of cider-making as well as a market for ironware brought up river from the Forest of Dean. Further north, the plains of Shropshire and Cheshire produced the greatest quantity of good cheese in England and sent it all round the country in the 16th century. So Shrewsbury had more than famous clothiers to its credit.

The damp, heavy soils of the west Midlands that produce good pasture also produce good oaks, and the timber buildings of the region are the most lavishly framed and the most ornate in all England. Beyond the Cotswolds, many of the building stones are forms of Triassic sandstone. Warm-tinted, though not always red, Triassic sandstone renders abundant, readily worked building material, but this easy virtue, which so quickly seduces the eye, is too soon despoiled by the weather. Along the Welsh borders there is a bewildering variety of different stones that vary in colour from dark red to pale blue, but by the 17th century fashion was turning to brick, a far better substitute for timber than most of the local stones.

Burford

OXFORDSHIRE

Many of the houses on the route leading down to the river contain medieval halls, and there are hints of this in their timber-framed walls, raised at a time when stone was still too expensive, even for the rich merchants here. By the 16th century stone was becoming more popular and cheaper. When the wool trade declined at the end of the century and wealth from coaching increased, an up-to-date appearance became important, so inns like The White Horse (BELOW) were given stone fronts.

WHEN the London–Cheltenham road was improved in 1812, it was diverted to the south of Burford. This set the seal on the town's long decline, and thankfully preserved it from the ravages of the next two centuries. The new road also gave Burford a dramatic new entry at the top of the High Street, instead of along the low road that followed the winding valley of the River Windrush. So Burford has survived as that rare thing, a medieval town of merchants' houses and inns.

Wool made Burford. The dry limestone of the Cotswolds was excellent for sheep pasture, and thousand-fold flocks had the run of the hills in the Middle Ages. The town and its wool merchants flourished. Between 1088 and 1107 one of the earliest merchants' guilds was established here, and an alderman and burgesses governed the town. Its earlier houses were built of timber and some of them are still visible, but many more are hidden because they were improved later on by the addition of facades in mellow Cotswold stone.

The 16th century brought the greatest wealth to the town with such clothiers as the Sylvesters, whose tombs are in the church. Another was Simon Wisdom, who founded the Grammar School in 1579. After the wool trade declined, coaching became the town's major source of wealth, so the inns continued to flourish – as they still do.

*Burford Bridge (*LEFT*) was built across the Windrush soon after 1323, and dramatically terminates the town at the bottom of the High Street, part of which is shown* BELOW.

*In Burford church (*LEFT*), on each side of the east window, are the accomplished monuments to Richard and Sarah Bartholomew (hers is shown* ABOVE*), who died in 1689.*

Chipping Campden

GLOUCESTERSHIRE

The High Street (BELOW) has a wonderful ensemble of houses, united by the fine qualities of Cotswold stone and the respect builders have always shown to its scale. Lining the street are typical burgage plots (see page 22) running back from the street, occasionally interspersed by narrow lanes. Where the street widens there is an island of buildings with the Market Hall, built by Sir Baptist Hicks (see page 96) in 1627. Its arcades (OPPOSITE) were at first intended only for the sale of cheese, butter and poultry.

CHIPPING CAMPDEN is the grandest of the Cotswold wool towns. Unlike Burford, it is not comprehensible all at a glance. The town has two parts, a small centre round the church representing the old village, and a curving High Street of constantly changing views. The church's spiky tower, glorifying wool as much as the faith, rises over the stone tiles of the town's countless roofs, which spread out in a profusion of honeyed tints pricked out with the greens and purples of mosses and lichens.

By 1247 Chipping Campden had a weekly market and three annual fairs. Its greatest medieval benefactor was William Grevel, commemorated as the 'flower of the wool merchants of all England'. His house is in the High Street and the brass to him and his wife in the church records his death in 1401. A further reminder of his time is Staplers' Hall, built for Robert Calf, another wool merchant. In the 15th century the cloth trade was in full swing, and bringing the profits that soon transformed the church into a model of Perpendicular Gothic.

These profits also built up the town, but, unlike Burford, Chipping Campden did not suffer decline together with cloth manufacture in the 16th century. Flax and silk weaving kept it going, and silver-smithing brought fresh wealth. Much of the town is therefore Georgian and the later buildings are a worthy successor to what wool had built in the Middle Ages.

The Elizabethan remains of Campden House (ABOVE) lie a good mile outside the town, its Victorian additions now all gone. It contrasts with the low houses of Sheep Street (LEFT) and the tightly packed houses of the High Street (RIGHT). Though Sheep Street obviously recalls the town's reliance on wool for its early prosperity, it demonstrates the town's later sources of wealth. Silk was manufactured here in the 18th century, and the old Silk Mill was where the architect C. R. Ashbee, attracted by the town's beauty, founded the Guild of Handicrafts at the beginning of this century. The mill is still occupied, but now by a family of silversmiths.

One of the town's great benefactors was Sir Baptist Hicks, who died in 1629. His miraculously precise tomb, showing him lying immaculately dressed beside his wife, was probably carved by the great mason Nicholas Stone. Hicks built the manor house, which was destroyed in the Civil War, but its gateway survives near the church. Just down Church Street are the gabled almshouses (ABOVE, RIGHT) he gave in 1612 for twelve poor persons of the town. Unlike his monument, the style of the almshouses is remarkably old fashioned.

The stylish gabled bay of William Grevel's house (OPPOSITE) was built towards the end of the 14th century. Its two storeys of windows set together in cusped panelling with a pair of gargoyles capping the angles are a rare survivor of the domestic architecture of the Middle Ages.

The contrast between the medieval tradition that lasted until the start of the 18th century and the Georgian classicism that followed is well shown by the mullions and hoodmould of the window ABOVE and in the plain sash windows and pedimented doorways on the RIGHT.

Cirencester

GLOUCESTERSHIRE

The Jurassic stone of the Cotswolds can be easily carved, and the vertical window bars (mullions) were usually given rounded mouldings. One of the great features of Cotswold stone is that some seams of it (called 'pendle') can be split into thin layers. These make excellent tiles that can be laid to sweep around valleys in the roof, so facilitating the construction of gables. The Venetian window of the house shown ABOVE, with its arched central light and flat frame, consequently sits oddly in this typical gable.

CIRENCESTER was the Roman Corinium, the administrative capital of south-west Britain. Here Ermine Street and Akeman Street had their junction with the Fosse Way and made the important crossing of the River Churn. Rich villas lay all about. To the south-east was the fertile cornland of the civil zone, north and west the stony Cotswolds and beyond that the military zone. But the Romans withdrew and their civilization collapsed. Corinium was abandoned and corpses were left to rot in its streets.

When Cirencester came to be rebuilt in the Middle Ages it never achieved the same importance – Bristol saw to that. Its streets kept to a gridiron plan, more or less, but the alignment was not quite the same as that of the Roman town, and many streets broke the pattern and led directly to the Market Place and the parish church beside it.

Cirencester became a small but flourishing market town, with wool, as always around the Cotswolds, as the basis of its early wealth. The Augustinians of Cirencester Abbey, now vanished but for Spital Gate outside the town, owned the sheep, but the merchants who traded in the wool profited and it was they who paid for one of the most sumptuous churches of the Cotswolds.

The church is as elaborately planned and carved (BELOW) as befitted the wealth of the clothiers who paid for it. The upper chamber of its elaborate south porch was used by the abbey's monks for secular business and, more ominously, for dealing with the royal commissioners who increasingly were casting envious eyes on all abbeys' finances in the trying years that led up to the Dissolution in 1539.

A century after the abbey had been suppressed, Cirencester's importance as a cloth town began to decline, but the market turned to other merchandise, especially the cattle and grain that an increasingly wealthy and growing population was demanding for its tables. The town, meanwhile, continued to renew its buildings, leaving a wide mixture of styles, with most of the older houses (RIGHT) belonging to the 17th and 18th centuries, when wool had been dethroned as the main source of wealth.

Great Malvern

WORCESTERSHIRE

In Wells Road, close by the Priory Church, there are several villas dating from the later 19th century. Unlike the earlier, classical houses, they are mostly Tudor or Jacobean in style, with aggressive mock timber-framing and bargeboarded gables alternating with shaped brick or stone gables, one of them completely shrouded in creeper (ABOVE) as though to hide too blatant a show of architectural revivalism.

So startling are the Malvern Hills that they were called the English Alps. A short string of hills does not make a mountain chain, but the Malvern Hills do make a prominent show. In the lee of this great outcrop that divides the Vales of Hereford and Worcester the Benedictines built two priories, a major one here, and, later, a lesser one further south at what became Little Malvern. At the Dissolution, Great Malvern preserved its Priory Church, now the only substantial medieval building amid much Victorian Gothic.

A small town grew up outside the walls of the greater priory, but it was of little consequence until, in 1756, a certain Dr Wall publicized the curative effects of the waters of Malvern Wells. Despite the fashion for baths and spas, it was still a long while before the present town was set on its course. In fact it was only the 19th century that brought the town some fame. The Pump Room and Baths were built 1819–23, and these attracted the young Princess Victoria here in 1830. The town then began the first phase of a course of expansion that came to a conclusion with the arrival of the railway in 1858.

The town's strong Victorian flavour is enhanced by the buildings of Malvern College, founded as a boys' public school in 1862, and by the former Imperial Hotel, now the Girls' College.

The earlier buildings, such as the Pump Room and the Foley Arms Hotel (BELOW), are stuccoed and classical. They were followed by rather more Italianate terraces and villas (seen from the hill, LEFT) and, by the middle of the century, the Tudor and Gothic styles were becoming firmly entrenched for new hotels, for the railway stations, and the later streets of houses. Now that the waters and the hydropathic cure are less fashionable, Malvern has become a dormitory for Worcester and Birmingham, and a good place for retirement, thanks to the qualities that brought the Benedictines here in the first place.

The Priory Church (LEFT) is an ornate example of the Perpendicular style, like Sherborne Abbey, though once again it masks much earlier work. Monastic churches were rarely rebuilt as thoroughly in the late Middle Ages as this was about 1420–60. The church consequently has typically large windows set into nave and choir, filling the entire gap between the buttresses, and a prominent crossing tower rising over them with overall panelling and large bell openings under the lacework of the battlemented and pinnacled parapet.

Ledbury

HEREFORDSHIRE

The parish church is reached from cobbled Church Lane (BELOW), which twists its way up the hill from the High Street. All the way up timber and brick intermingle. Many of the houses are daubed and plastered between the members of their timber frames, but a few have brick nogging instead, and there are several early jettied houses, such as this fine three-storeyed one, which has a projecting gabled oriel in the centre.

LEDBURY lies tucked into the western, Herefordshire side of the Malvern Hills where they are already falling towards the Vale of Gloucester. The town has a broad High Street that was probably laid out by one of the Bishops of Hereford, the lords of the town. Ledbury gains much of its character from the way this street runs along the foot of the steep slope that leads up towards the hills. Precipitous lanes run into the High Street and so does the main road from the east. There is a tight crossing and, to the north, the High Street widens in a most satisfactory way to make a site for an ancient market.

Numerous strikingly black and white timber-framed houses line the streets. This exaggerated contrast is a result of the timber being tarred in the 19th century, but the way the upper walls are split up into a series of identical square panels by timber studs is a traditional method of decoration in the west Midlands. The timber buildings are interspersed with others of bright red Hereford brick. Apart from the parish church, just one building used the local rosy red sandstone. This is the chapel of St Katherine's Hospital, built for the poor and infirm in the 14th century with a traceried window facing on to the High Street. Right at the northern end of the town is the impressive brick viaduct, built in 1859–61 to carry the railway from Great Malvern to Hereford.

Abbot's Lodge

Ledbury's market place is formed by the widening of its High Street. Jutting out into it are the arcades of the prominently decorated mid-17th-century timber-framed Market House (FAR LEFT). The buildings along the High Street are tightly packed as space was scarce, and gardens (LEFT) are usually long and narrow to fit the burgage plots.

The town has several fine 16th-century timber-framed inns. The Feathers Hotel (ABOVE) has an ornate front with close-set decorative studding forming long rectangles as well as squares, second only to the Market House in its impact on the High Street. The Prince of Wales in Church Lane (LEFT) is an altogether more modest building, dominated by the jetty of the adjacent Old Grammar School of about 1500, seen here to the right.

103

Ludlow

SHROPSHIRE

Broad Street runs down from the Butter Market to Broad Gate (OPPOSITE, BELOW RIGHT) at the bottom, with raised cobbled pavements above a roadway that finally narrows to pass through a gateway in the town walls. De Grey's famous café (BELOW) and splendidly varied houses contrast with numerous alleys (BOTTOM), especially those around the Butter Cross (OPPOSITE, BELOW LEFT).

LUDLOW owes its origin to the strategic value of its dramatic site. It lies above a steep cliff facing towards Wales. At the foot of the cliff is the River Teme, which, with a tributary, engirdles the town on three sides. The Anglo-Saxons used the site long before Roger de Montgomery or perhaps Roger de Lacy founded the castle here about 1086 to protect the Marches (the borderlands) against the Welsh and, as importantly, against the acquisitive attentions of other Norman lords.

Early in the 12th century the town was laid out on a carefully planned grid of streets to the south and east of the castle (*overleaf*), and in 1233 the town walls were started. After Edward I conquered the Welsh at the end of the century, the castle was made the palace of successive Princes of Wales. Ludlow became one of the strongest towns of the Marches, and one of the richest. This is immediately apparent in the size of the parish church, the largest in Shropshire, paid for out of the wealth brought by wool and the cloth industry. The work was prompted by the burgesses and numerous trade guilds. This prosperity did not outlast the Middle Ages, but soon after Elizabeth came to the throne in 1558 things improved. The castle had become the seat of the Lords President of Wales and their Council of the Marches met here, making Ludlow virtually the capital of Wales. Service industries flocked to the town and brought fresh wealth and the building of many inns.

The Council was eventually abolished in 1689, and when Defoe visited the town in the 1720s he found the castle 'the very perfection of decay'. But he thought Ludlow was a 'tolerable place', and so did the county's gentry, for whom it remained a fashionable social centre.

The Feathers (TOP), a mass of decorative timberwork, started as a house, possibly built for Thomas Hackluit, a secretary to the Council of the Marches. It was rebuilt early in the 17th century and became an inn only about 1660.

OVERLEAF: Ludlow from the west, spread out between castle and church.

Ludlow church is impressively built, and lavishly fitted out with stained glass, monuments and furnishings. The medieval seats in the stalls are fitted with misericords, decorated props for the clergy to ease long periods when they have to stand. They are carved with some marvellously satirical subjects, for instance an ale-wife carried off by a demon and a fox in bishop's robes preaching to geese. Then there is a mermaid (ABOVE) flanked by a pair of scaly fish. The feathered morris dancers (RIGHT) in Castle Square could well have stepped off another misericord. The rectangular grid of streets between the castle and the church (OPPOSITE) is most comprehensively seen from the top of the church tower. In the foreground are Hosyer's Almshouses, an expansive range built in 1758 round an open courtyard.

Much Wenlock

SHROPSHIRE

The town has nothing to show on the scale of the Priory buildings. It is, rather, the solid charm of oak timbering, warm tinted stone and brick (ABOVE, RIGHT) and stucco (ABOVE, FAR RIGHT), laid out along the intersecting St Mary's Lane, Bull Ring and Sheinton Street, that gives Much Wenlock its character.

The timber-framed Guildhall (BELOW, RIGHT), arcaded below and jettied out above, contrasts with the nearby Georgian brick houses. The stone part of the arcading at the rear is probably late medieval but the rest was built in 1577. The hall upstairs has Jacobean panelling and a fine timber roof (BELOW, LEFT), with curved braces supporting tie-beams and raking struts that reach up to the roof rafters in the typical local manner.

MUCH WENLOCK lies at the northern end of Wenlock Edge, the curious geological ribbon of Silurian shales and limestone that juts out diagonally across the Shropshire landscape to form one of its most characteristic features. These hills inspired the poet A. E. Housman to write *A Shropshire Lad*, which provided the texts for *On Wenlock Edge*, one of the finest and best-loved works of the composer and collector of folksongs Ralph Vaughan Williams.

The town owes its origin to St Mildburga who founded a convent here about 690, and became its first abbess. Twice the convent was destroyed and once the nuns were restored to it. Then, after the Conquest, the powerful Earl Roger de Montgomery made it into a Priory and brought monks from Cluny in France to occupy it. They built a fine church and extensive conventual buildings, set round a cloister. Among these was a *lavatorium*, where the monks washed before meals. It survives as a rare reminder of monastic life, and some decorative arcading belonging to the church also survived the despoliation brought by the Dissolution of the Monasteries. The town, though small, had its own church, and so, when the Priory was suppressed, its church was not spared, but allowed to decay into the picturesque ruins of today. Luckily one part of the Priory, its lodge, was valued and became a house. This building, overlooking the ruins of the past, is of great significance in the history of English domestic architecture and a fine example of a lodging of about 1500.

The ruins of Wenlock Priory (ABOVE) consist of part of the east wall of the transept, on the left, with three chapels opening off it; the bases of the columns of the nave arcade, in the middle; and the southern side of the west front, to the left. These superseded a narrower Norman nave uncovered by excavation.

The most prominent house in the High Street is Ashfield House (LEFT), with an early Tudor ground storey of stone, carrying prominent timber-framed gables and tall, fluted chimney-stacks added later.

Ross-on-Wye

HEREFORDSHIRE

R OSS-ON-WYE, said Daniel Defoe, is 'a good old town, famous for good cider, a great manufacture of iron ware, and a good trade on the River Wye'. It is built memorably on a cliff of red sandstone overlooking a sweeping bend in the river, with the church spire set over it like a gigantic exclamation mark.

In the town itself, the hill dominates most of the views. The High Street climbs up from the river past red sandstone facades, occasionally broken by timber-framing, to reach the Market Place. Along the way are the low, red sandstone Rudhall almshouses, founded in 1575 by one of the family whose monuments have a prominent position in the church. Among the timber buildings are the Saracen's Head and a terrace that includes Kyrle's House (*below*).

This house has an importance out of proportion to its size, for here lived John Kyrle, the town's greatest benefactor, a man who would have been forgotten had not the poet Alexander Pope praised him for his dedication to the landscape. Kyrle devoted his wealth to providing the town with a public garden, called The Prospect, which he acquired in 1693, and laid out with two classical gates dated 1700 to mark its entrances. While much of the planting within The Prospect has been lost, the fine view from here out across the river towards the Vale of Hereford is still as enticing as ever.

The High Street (BELOW) is constricted by the Market House, on the right, which stands out opposite a fine range of three-storeyed timber-framed houses, with decorative close-studding and later, inserted sash windows. One of these houses became The King's Arms. Coleridge stayed there in 1794 and wrote of its former inhabitant, 'Richer than miser o'er his countless hoards, Nobler than kings or king-polluted lords, Here dwelt the man of Ross.' This was none other than John Kyrle.

The Market House (ABOVE) was built of sandstone about 1660–74 in the usual way over an arcade of solid, round columns and heavy piers at each end. Pairs of round-headed windows run down the side and one of the gabled ends carries a medallion of Charles II. Over the roof there is a pretty clock tower. The interior is divided by an arcade of tapering timber piers running down the axis of the hall.

From the river, the view of the town is dominated by the tall point of the church spire and trees all along the skyline (RIGHT). To this day The Prospect, to the far right of the picture, also gives Ross its leafy aspect from the river, but since 1836 a road has run beneath the garden. The white stucco and gables of the Royal Hotel appeared the next year. Fanciful embattled walls and a tower followed, and they give the town all the appearance of ancient fortifications. The hotel (ABOVE, RIGHT) stands out plain and white, with wavy bargeboards and standard sash windows, all fashionable in their day but a little out of tune with the older buildings of the town.

Shrewsbury

SHROPSHIRE

Sʜʀᴇᴡsʙᴜʀʏ combines all the virtues of a medieval country town with some of the finest early monuments of the Industrial Revolution – a rare accomplishment.

The town lies on a hill in a great loop of the River Severn, with a castle, also one of Roger de Montgomery's works, placed high in the narrow neck of land to defend it.

Shrewsbury is said to have been founded by refugees from Wroxeter, the Roman town of Viroconium, when they were looking for security as Rome collapsed. Five miles upstream from Viroconium they came upon the site they needed, easily defensible and strategically commanding the fertile Shropshire Plain. Monks and merchants found it ideal. Wool and milk brought them wealth. In the 18th century Shrewsbury did well as a staging post on the turnpike road from London to Holyhead.

When coal and iron were exploited down the Severn at Coalbrookdale, Shrewsbury became one of the earliest places to employ iron in the construction of its buildings. In 1796 it saw the world's first iron-framed building ever to be erected, a flax mill, serving one of the town's important industries that were taking the place of the old woollen business. The mill was a worthy though less ostentatious successor to the great timber mansions built for wealthy wool merchants such as Robert Ireland and Richard Owen.

It is surprising in a town built on so constricted a site to find plenty of open space, most of all by a river that was a lifeline for trade. Nevertheless the wide lawns of The Quarry (ABOVE) running up from the Severn are Shrewsbury's principal park. They were laid out in 1719, with the quarry itself converted into The Dingle in 1879. Many buildings in the town are closely set together, but again they invariably contrast with open spaces, such as around Bear Steps (RIGHT) which leads up to the churchyard of St Alkmund's. Here medieval timber and stonework combine with the accretions of five hundred years to give the town one of its most intriguing intimate views.

The Presbyterian church (LEFT) of 1870 rises monstrously above Castle Gates House, rebuilt here in 1702. Claremont Bank (BELOW) offers further contrasts in its early 19th-century houses.

The ancient church of St Chad collapsed in 1788, and a new one was built in 1790–2 by George Steuart, with a prominent western tower and a rotunda for the galleried nave (LEFT). Another view of Bear Steps is ABOVE.

115

Stratford-upon-Avon

WARWICKSHIRE

*Next to the Guildhall are the Almshouses
(ABOVE), built about 1427 with a long front,
since lengthened. They are typical of many of
Stratford's timber-framed buildings in
having close-set, decorative studs
exemplifying conspicuous consumption of
timber. The main structural timbers are
marked out by their slightly greater width and
the curved brackets that support the jetty
above. All the windows have been restored,
but their positions immediately under the
jetty and the roof are exactly right.*

THERE is no escaping it: the gently flowing Avon, which attracted settlers
in the Bronze Age, which watered a Romano-British village, which gave
Anglo-Saxon monks a balmy site for a monastery, which, in short, gave
Stratford all the advantages that any town might need, is Shakespeare's
river. Even so, 'by this river', Defoe recorded, 'they drive a very great trade
for sugar, oil, wine, tobacco, iron, lead, and in a word all heavy goods' up to
Stratford, and in return Stratford merchants sent corn and especially cheese
down to Bristol.

In 1196 the Bishop of Worcester gave Stratford the right to hold a market.
The town became independent, eventually being governed by the powerful
Guild of the Holy Cross. In 1417 the Guild built themselves a hall, or, rather,
two halls, one over the other, beside the chapel that they had founded
before 1296 and would rebuild soon afterwards. The Guildhall later became
the Grammar School where Shakespeare was probably taught in the 1570s.
One of the Guild's most influential members, Sir Hugh Clopton, whose
chapel is in the parish church, was responsible for the Clopton Bridge of
1480–90, just before he became Lord Mayor of London. In the 16th century
the Guild was succeeded by a bailiff and aldermen. One of the bailiffs was
called John Shakespeare; he was William's father.

When Defoe visited Stratford, he went to see 'the monument of old Shakespear, the famous poet' in Holy Trinity Church (RIGHT) on the southern fringes of the town. That was at the start of the 18th century, long before the actor David Garrick held the first Shakespeare festival here in 1769, and started Stratford on its new career as England's greatest tourist attraction outside London.

Everywhere there are reminders of Shakespeare. In 1597 Shakespeare bought New Place for his retirement, a house later occupied by Thomas Nash, who married Shakespeare's grand-daughter. In the 18th century the house was demolished by its owner because he was tired of the constant stream of visitors, but the garden (BELOW, LEFT) is preserved. To the west of the town at Shottery is Anne Hathaway's Cottage (BELOW, RIGHT), the home of the family of Shakespeare's wife. It comprises a medieval hall and east wing, and additions to the west made after Shakespeare's time. The ornate front of Harvard House (BELOW, CENTRE), built in 1596 immediately after a major fire in the town, makes a change from the dour close-studding of the Guildhall and Almshouses.

117

Tewkesbury

GLOUCESTERSHIRE

Down by the Avon is the site of the abbey mill, though the present mill (BELOW) dates from early in the 19th century. It is said to have been the inspiration for Abel Fletcher's mill in Mrs Craik's John Halifax, Gentleman. *At all events, it is now a restaurant, proud of this and its 12th-century origin. St Mary's Lane (OPPOSITE) frames a view of the medieval terrace in Church Street. Its likely connection with the abbey is neatly symbolized by the presence of the tower behind.*

TEWKESBURY lies at the lower end of the Vale of Evesham where the Warwickshire Avon meets the River Severn. This is rich countryside, fertile, sheltered and mild. There were monks here at the start of the 8th century, but it was not until the beginning of the 12th century that the great Benedictine Abbey was founded. Because of the rivers and their smaller tributaries, Tewkesbury has a constricted site, with three main streets of shops and houses. Alleys run between them and go down to quays by the river. In the 11th century a market was established where the streets join.

Every bit of space had to be exploited. This meant narrow frontages and much building to the rear. It was a natural place to build terraces. So it is that Tewkesbury has one of the oldest terraces and certainly the longest and best-conserved medieval terrace in the country (*right*). It was almost certainly built by the monks, as a speculation, against the north side of the precinct. One of the individual houses has been opened as a museum to show how a hall, shop and bedroom could be fitted into the tight space.

For the most part, though, Tewkesbury was built up with individual shops, inns and houses. They come in a bewildering array of styles. Medieval timber-framing, often complete with cusped windows and much carving, jostles for space beside elegant Georgian brick fronts, replete with classical detailing, in an ever-changing medley of shapes.

The Town Hall originated in a building of 1788 that was enlarged about 1840 and then taken in hand in 1891. This produced an attractive facade with round-headed windows set between Tuscan columns supporting an entablature and pediment. It makes a good backdrop for civic splendour: here the mayor takes the salute of a local regiment.

The pair of jettied shops ABOVE, in Church Street, was perhaps built shortly after the medieval terrace opposite them and they are a good deal more ornate. Their three storeys were nevertheless probably used in much the same way, as shops as well as domestic rooms.

The Baptist Chapel set in a court off Church Street is among the oldest nonconformist chapels in the country (LEFT). It was built in 1623 to provide a room for meetings and preaching, and so was very different from medieval churches, where ritual determined the plan. The Church of England was nevertheless moving in the same direction and most late 17th-century churches were principally designed as auditoriums for preaching. The layout of the furnishings still differentiates nonconformist chapels – for instance, the central position of the minister's pulpit, visible here, which was added later in the century, together with the gallery.

The south side of the abbey (ABOVE) was originally filled with the conventual buildings. The splendid church is equally famous for its Norman arcading and intricate 14th-century vaulting. At the Dissolution the citizens of the town valued it so much that they purchased it. Its plan, with a polygonal apse at the east end and six chapels radiating from it, was once common in abbey churches, and admirably suited to monks who had to attend mass every day and needed many altars for private prayer. It was nevertheless this part that the parish first occupied, leaving the open, Norman nave to remain disused for a long time.

The Royal Hop Pole Hotel (ABOVE) in Church Street, like many other buildings in Tewkesbury, is a refronting of an older building. The facade, in painted brick, belongs to the late 18th century, when timber framing was despised as old fashioned. The new front has a wide porch that welcomes visitors with a dry greeting. The timber building next door to the right is again part of the hotel, and might also have been refronted if there had been more money. As it is, it satisfyingly maintains the constantly changing street line so characteristic of the town.

At the corner of Church Street and Tolzey Lane is Cross House (RIGHT), so called because it stands close to where the Market Cross used to be. It was probably built in the 15th century and at the time must have been among the finest of Tewkesbury's timber-framed houses. It is unusually tall, with three full storeys and a lofty garret. The Tolzey Lane side bends round to follow the street, marking its progress with three large gables. They and the jetties below them give the lane its dark, mysterious feeling, with the light at the end marking Church Street in a particularly magnetic way.

Warwick

WARWICKSHIRE

From the river, Warwick is dominated by the castle (BELOW), yet from within the town, the castle is in the background or not visible at all. It was founded in 1068 by William the Conqueror, though what can be seen today is mostly the work of the Earls of Warwick in the 14th and 15th centuries. From its ramparts can be seen the timber houses of Mill Street, part of the town to escape the fire of 1694.

WARWICK is famous for its magnificent castle. But, reported the antiquary John Leland about 1540, 'The beauty and glory of the towne is in two streets, whereof the one is caullyd Highe Streete and goith from the east gate to the west . . . the other crossithe the middle of it, makynege Quadrivium, and goithe from northe to southe.' Most people think of the castle first, though the town is far older. It was founded in 914 as a *burh* (see page 12) by King Alfred's daughter Ethelfleda, the so-called 'Lady of the Mercians', as a defensive stronghold against the Danes. The site on a rocky spur of Carboniferous Limestone overlooking the Avon was ideal, and, though the Danes were not kept at bay, the town flourished.

The town Leland praised was burnt in 1694, but when Celia Fiennes visited it a few years later rebuilding had already made it 'regular and fine', with many buildings of 'brick and coyn'd [quoined] with stone and the windows the same'. Defoe, who saw it twenty years later still, found it 'rebuilt in so noble and so beautiful a manner, that few towns in England make so fine an appearance'.

That is still clear in the fine tower of the parish church, as much a landmark as the castle, and the civic buildings and terraces of houses that lie to its north. Nevertheless much was spared by the fire on the south side of the town, including a number of timber-framed houses and the town gates.

The Leycester Hospital (TOP, LEFT AND RIGHT) is a combination of 15th-century timber-framed guild buildings and 16th-century houses that was taken over as almshouses for the Earl of Leicester's foundation of 1571, with a galleried courtyard (LEFT) decorated with a heraldic porcupine. In the Beauchamp Chapel of the church is an extraordinarily lifelike gilded brass effigy of Richard Beauchamp, Earl of Warwick, who died in 1439. It shows him recumbent in prayer, with a heraldic bear (ABOVE) and griffin at his feet.

Lakeland and the Peaks

CUMBRIA · DERBYSHIRE
YORKSHIRE

UNTIL the Industrial Revolution, the north-west, for all its beauty, was the poorest region of England. Its climate is drenchingly wet, its summers are short – so far as there are any. The Pennines are bleak, the Cumbrian Mountains more bleak still and soaking. The valleys are tight and cold, the plains few, and then soggy underfoot.

Apart from the red sandstones continuing into the valleys of the north-west from the west Midlands, much of the stone here is as dark as the climate. The Carboniferous stones of the Pennines and the even harder Ordovician and Silurian stones and, above all, the granites of Cumbria, make a number of subtle variations in colours, where black is never far out of mind. This was no place to encourage wealth.

To make matters worse, the northern counties were disputed territory, and peace with the Scots, never achieved for long by the Romans, only came with the Union of the Crowns in 1603. Then the north-west began to catch up. Industries like weaving, which long since had made towns rich further south, provided modest prosperity, but no town, not even Carlisle, became a wealthy administrative centre for the Borders, as Ludlow was for the Marches. In the 18th century, thankfully, other qualities began to be appreciated. In an increasingly populous nation, the loneliness and the dramatic beauty of the landscape impressed romantic minds. Just as the Industrial Revolution was turning the Lancashire Plain into a battlefield between new technology and the labouring masses to the immense benefit of the nation, Wordsworth and Coleridge found their escape not very far north in the Lakeland of Cumbria, and nourished the language with their verse.

Soon the mining and farming that gave a few towns some prosperity were joined by tourism, as visitors came in search of curative waters, stupendous views and vigorous walks. They were the making of towns as far apart as Buxton and Keswick, seen here against the magnificent backdrop of Derwent Water.

Appleby

CUMBRIA

Boroughgate (ABOVE) curves slightly as it runs from the castle down to the church. The street acts as the market place and is marked by two Tuscan columns, High Cross and Low Cross, as well as by the Moot Hall of 1596, set on an island site. There are a number of plain 18th-century houses and several Victorian Gothic buildings.

APPLEBY lies in the valley of the Eden, the river that divides the high moors of the Pennines from the higher mountains of the Lake District. Above the town to the east is the old Roman road that used to run to the west end of Hadrian's Wall.

The town was fought over, especially by the Scots after its transfer to England in 1052, and they laid it waste in 1388, but the town survived, thanks to its good communications and its sheltered position, which spares it from the worst of Cumbria's rain.

Appleby itself is not one but two, divided by the river. Old Appleby lies on the east and carries the main road between Richmond and Penrith. New Appleby was founded over the bridge about 1100 with a small grid of streets centred on Boroughgate. The castle was started by the Viponts as a motte and at least three baileys in the 12th century. It was enlarged by the Cliffords, and domesticated in 1686-8 by the Earl of Thanet, the son-in-law of Lady Anne, the last of the Cliffords. She left her mark on the town by restoring the parish church and building the chapel that contains her tomb, as well as by restoring the medieval church of St Michael, which she proudly claimed to have 'raised from its ruins', and founding St Anne's Hospital in 1657.

The view from the castle (ABOVE) shows how closely Appleby's houses keep to the shelter of the trees that line the Eden valley, and how soon the hills rise above them as a prelude to the high moors, which are only two or three miles away.

Though the Moot Hall was built as a Market Hall in 1596, it was refronted in the 18th century, rendered and painted white, and given a sound roof of Westmorland slate. Over the southern end there is a small bellcote (RIGHT), like a chapel's.

Bakewell

DERBYSHIRE

From the northern edge of Bakewell, streets of stone houses (ABOVE), built of the local iron-grey Carboniferous limestone, pile down into the centre of town. Behind them is the valley of the Wye and, immediately beyond, the hills start rising again in a profusion of green. The valleys of the Peak make excellent pasture for cattle to complement the rough grazing on the moors, which only sheep can brave in all seasons.

Bakewell is an ancient market town set in the narrow valley of the Derbyshire Wye at the foot of the steep hills of the Peak. The bridge was built about 1300, but the shaft of a Saxon cross at the church shows much earlier occupation, and the moors around are covered in prehistoric barrows. The church, overlooking the town, is one of the most ambitious in the region, and suggests that the comparatively sheltered and fertile valley made the town unusually rich for this part of the country.

Celia Fiennes called Bakewell 'a pretty neate market town' when she saw it in 1697. The gabled Market Hall was then new, like many other buildings that give the town its present character. That, too, was the year in which the Duke of Rutland, the owner of nearby Haddon Hall, built the Bath House. Oddly Celia Fiennes did not mention this, nor the warm springs. She was a devotee of spas, and the 'well' in 'Bakewell' refers to the spring, so she could hardly have missed it.

The 'Bake', incidentally, does not refer to the puddings or tarts that have made the town a household word. They came into existence by mistake in the kitchens of the Rutland Arms hotel. This is an attractive building of 1804, which is also distinguished for a room in which Jane Austen is said to have written part of *Pride and Prejudice*.

The market at Bakewell (ABOVE) in full course, with moorland sheep a topic of vital and lengthy consideration. There is more money in them than in Bakewell puddings. Even so, since 1859 the puddings have been on sale in a shop (LEFT) opposite the hotel where they were first made. They were invented when the cook misinterpreted her mistress's recipe, and, instead of mixing the egg into the pastry and filling the tart with jam, put the jam into the tart and poured the egg mixture over it. The result was an instant success and the puddings are now the local speciality.

Buxton

DERBYSHIRE

In the 1780s the fifth duke employed the architect John Carr of York to develop Buxton with Royal Crescent (BELOW), which contains the Assembly Rooms. It has a grand classical form, with a rusticated, round-arched arcade supporting giant fluted pilasters that embrace the main storeys and terminate in an entablature and balustraded parapet. It is the architectural centrepiece of the town, and was soon followed by terraces of grand houses and stabling close by.

LIKE Tunbridge Wells, Buxton is a spa. Unlike Tunbridge Wells, it has ancient origins, and its waters are clear, sweet, bluish and warm. Buxton was on the road that the Romans built across the Pennine moorland leading to Brough and the north-west, and they established a fort nearby. But they also noticed the waters springing from the depths of the hard Carboniferous limestone, and they named the place Aquae Arnemetiae.

Hardly any of that survives today. Though pilgrims came in the Middle Ages seeking miraculous cures and the waters very much remained in favour in Elizabethan times, Buxton became a market town and turned its back on people seeking the cure. Defoe complained of this, though the waters had a good reputation as a cure for 'rheumatic, scorbutic and scrofulous distempers, aches of the joints, nervous pains, and also in scurvy and leprous maladies'. The trouble was that the baths were overcrowded and visitors found it difficult to find accommodation. The only place for them was in The Hall, which the Earl of Shrewsbury had erected over the baths in about 1570. This state of affairs continued until the fifth Duke of Devonshire, lord of the manor of Buxton, decided to make the town into a real spa and extend what was already England's highest market town further up the valley towards the high moors.

Once St Anne's Well (TOP RIGHT) was hung with the crutches of pilgrims. The water was 'not unpleasant but rather like milk', recorded Celia Fiennes. At the centre of Carr's Buxton lay the Great Stables, with a large circular courtyard for riding. In 1878 this was given a large iron dome for a hospital, and the town its most prominent landmark (TOP LEFT). The sixth and seventh dukes continued to develop Buxton, and it is nowadays by no means just a spa; it is a place to visit for music at the Pavilion and Opera House (LEFT AND ABOVE), designed by Frank Matcham, the most successful theatre architect of the day, in 1903. Buxton remains the centre of the Peak, where, in Defoe's words, 'there is healthy country, a great variety of view to satisfy the curious, and fine down or moor for the ladies to take a ring upon in their coaches . . .'

133

Keswick

CUMBRIA

Greta Hall was new when Coleridge lived there, and is now part of Keswick School. The Town Hall in Main Street is a rather later Georgian building that dates from 1813 and looks a bit like a church with a tower at one end. The parish church was built in the 19th century in the Gothic style among plain but pretty Georgian houses (ABOVE), many of which are rendered and painted to reduce the overwhelming effect of the dark stone.

Keswick is built from the darkest of grey stones, the hard Ordovician sandstone. This rises up behind the town to Skiddaw, the third highest of the Cumbrian peaks after the Sca Fell Pikes and Helvyllyn. It gives Keswick its character and also the greatest rainfall in England. But despite this and the ubiquitous sombre hues, Keswick is the prettiest of towns, delightfully set above deep, dark Derwent Water and the narrow plain that leads across to Bassenthwaite Lake.

The poet Thomas Gray spent six days here in 1769 'lap'd in Elysium'. Later, Keswick attracted all the Lakeland poets. Coleridge came to live at Greta Hall in 1800 and stayed with his family to enjoy its beautiful views until severe colds sent him away in 1803. Charles Lamb, who hated the countryside, brought his sister to visit the Coleridges and the two of them spent three 'delightful weeks' there. Southey went to live there too, and died in the house in 1843. William and Dorothy Wordsworth, who lived over the way at Grasmere, spent a holiday at the Royal Oak Hotel. Shelley came for a while and numerous other writers followed.

With such predecessors as these, and so much grand scenery all around, it is no wonder that Keswick attracts visitors in droves, despite being the wettest town in England.

The oldest building in Keswick is the church behind the town at Crosthwaite, which is dedicated to St Kentigern, the Cumbrian missionary. This is where Southey is buried. The most recent buildings are semi-detached houses, plain or fanciful, on the edge of the slope up to Skiddaw, and the cinema (LEFT), in a style as much to do with Moorish Spain as with Keswick.

Kirkby Lonsdale

CUMBRIA

The aisles of the church were among the last parts built, and have standardized Perpendicular windows (ABOVE, LEFT), with pairs of trefoiled windows set under straight-headed hoodmoulds. The churchyard is enclosed on two sides by the backs of houses (ABOVE, RIGHT), but on the other side there is a gazebo. It faces up the valley (OPPOSITE): 'one of the loveliest scenes in England – therefore in the world', wrote John Ruskin. His passions were the Alps and Gothic architecture, so he should have known.

Lonsdale is the narrow valley cut by the River Lune through the fells of the western edge of the Pennines. Kirkby is the town of the kirk, the church of St Mary.

Outside, the church has evidence of money spent on it over a long period, starting with an ornate Norman doorway at the west end, and continuing with all the styles of Gothic to produce a very enjoyable patina. Inside, the church is a wonderful surprise, with a great arcade of stout Norman piers, incised with patterns in the style of Durham Cathedral. They are confined to one side of the church, and stop short, their purpose unfulfilled. The church was probably paid for, so far as it was built, out of the wealth brought by the sheep raised on the fells, and, later, by weaving cloth from their wool, but what the original intentions of its builders were and why they were not brought to their conclusion is quite obscure. Nonetheless this can never have been a particularly prosperous town.

The town has little else to show of early wealth, perhaps unsurprisingly, and the rest of the town is quite modest. From the church, the Main Street runs past dark grey but welcoming stone houses to reach the fine Manor House of about 1700. Nearby is the 15th-century Devil's Bridge, traditionally built by Satan himself, with three ribbed arches rising from pointed cut-waters to span the River Lune.

At the far end of the Market Square is the Savings Bank (FAR RIGHT), built about 1840 in a rather severe classical style, relieved by a small, open turret. Fountain House (RIGHT), by comparison, is much more outgoing. Perhaps built as late as 1700, it has old-fashioned but impressive cross-framed windows and a central doorway flanked by Ionic columns.

Settle

NORTH YORKSHIRE

O N Langcliffe Scar above Settle there are caves that housed palaeolithic hunters during the Ice Age. In Settle itself there is little, even of the Middle Ages, to suggest much antiquity. Yet its attractive riverside setting near the head of Ribblesdale must have been chosen for strategic reasons, and was to become a good market place long before tourists came for the scenery. From the 12th century the great Yorkshire monasteries kept large flocks of sheep on the moors and herded cattle in the valleys. The wool was sold direct, but cheese and to a lesser extent meat needed a local market, and Settle provided one.

Little of that is evident now. A number of pleasant Georgian houses gives the town its character today, together with the 17th-century Shambles in the Market Square, and one of Yorkshire's earliest Meeting Houses, built modestly by the Quakers in 1678.

The strangely carved lintel of The Folly's doorway, in the High Street, takes a northern tradition to an extreme. In Yorkshire especially, doorways were the one place where masons always felt they should provide some decoration. The hard Pennine stone resisted their chisels to such an extent that carving had to be restricted to where it would have the greatest effect, and so they often made doorways into works of art and inscribed them with the date and the owner's initials.

At the end of the High Street is The Folly (ABOVE), not named because it pretends to be what it is not, like most follies, nor because of the capricious detailing, but because its builder, Thomas Preston, over-reached himself and ran out of money before he had completed it. The fantastic doorway, dated 1679, is flanked by columns like overblown drumsticks, and the lintel has a pair of pointed arches like eyebrows raised in the utmost surprise. The jeweller's shop (TOP) is in the Market Place. Up the slope is School Hill (RIGHT), with walls and steps as rugged as the local stone.

Another traditional carved doorway (RIGHT) lies at the end of an alley near the end of the Market Place. The pair of flat double curves of its lintel bearing the date are typical of 17th-century Pennine houses and can be seen by the dozen in towns and on farms alike. Standing out from the stone tiles and slates of the Market Place (BELOW), the gables of the Elizabethan-style Town Hall of 1832 maintain the local tradition of building, even though the craftsmanship is now stiffening with old age. The bookshop window (FAR RIGHT) fills a small building in the High Street.

Castles and Dales

DURHAM · HUMBERSIDE
NORTHUMBERLAND
YORKSHIRE

Though colder than the north-west, the north-east is neither so wet nor so confined by high mountains. The plains had a good agricultural potential that was understood by prehistoric settlers and then by the Romans who made Eboracum, the present York, a bastion against unsubdued tribes further north. Nevertheless the north-east remained disputed territory and a centre of insurrection. It was left to William the Conqueror to make it his own, and then only by a brutal show of arms, which laid waste the land for his barons and new monasteries to colonize. Edward I attempted to remove the threat of the Scots by conquest, but they remained a problem until the Union of the Crowns in 1603.

If towns were to survive they needed good defences, as the walls of York still show. With them they might become far more prosperous than the towns of the north-west. York itself became a provincial capital and one of the largest towns in the country after London, but lesser towns such as Helmsley (*left*) did well as bastions against invasion and centres of trade that served great monastic estates. With much moorland in the region, sheep were a necessary source of wealth, and Beverley flourished through trading in wool. Weaving, though, was never so important as on the western side of the country, but stockings, hand-knitted in countless homes, were a valuable enough commodity for trade to give Richmond a market set aside especially for their sale.

As in most of the north, there was little good building timber, and many lowly buildings had to rely on earthen walls supported by thin saplings until brick and stone became cheap in the 17th century. The hard Carboniferous stones of the Pennines contrast with more amenable limestone in the North Yorkshire Moors, rather porous limestone along the west side of the Vale of York, and sandstone of various qualities. Large parts of the region had nothing but clay, so brick making was developed remarkably early, especially around Hull and Beverley.

Alnwick

NORTHUMBERLAND

ALNWICK is forever linked with the house of Percy, the great medieval family who controlled much of the north-east. The castle, though, was founded before their time, perhaps soon after the Conquest by Gilbert de Tesson, Willam's standard-bearer at the Battle of Hastings. Around 1100 his timber and earthen castle was in the hands of Yvo de Vescy, and he built in stone. But it was in 1309 that Henry de Percy purchased the castle and started building in earnest. There was a pressing need. Edward I had failed to conquer the Scots, and if Northumberland were to be held it had to have strong castles.

There had been long periods when there was an accommodation with the Scots. This is testified by the ruins of the chapel of St Leonard's Hospital, founded between 1193 and 1216 for the benefit of the soul of Malcolm, King of Scotland, killed at the siege of Alnwick in 1093. Peace seldom lasted for long, and so the town itself had to have strong defences. Fortifications were eventually licensed in 1424, and they brought to the town the plain and stolid Hotspur Gate. Inside the walls the scene changes to handsomely paved streets of fine 18th-century houses, for instance in Bondgate Within and its continuation, the well-named curving Narrowgate. Like everything else in the town, they use the hard stone of central Northumberland.

The Georgian style of most of the buildings in Alnwick belongs to the same taste that once could be seen in the remodelled castle and still can be in many of the monuments in its grounds. There is a defensive quality in the iron-dark Carboniferous limestone of the houses within the walls of the town that unites them with the past, and gives them a hard face despite their handsome proportions and polite detailing. The end of Narrowgate is shown ABOVE; the handsome three-storeyed house on the RIGHT is in Bailiffgate, which is also shown OPPOSITE.

The castle's medieval associations are more romantic than real. In the 18th century it was thoroughly domesticated in the Palladian classical taste, but the fourth Duke of Northumberland found it both uncomfortable and far too insipid. From 1854 he employed the 19th century's greatest castle architect, Anthony Salvin, to bring the interiors up to the best standard of the day with a lavish suite of Italianate state rooms, and to return the exterior to a proper semblance of a medieval castle (RIGHT). This he did, not through archaeological reconstruction, but through vivid imaginative re-creation that, by comparison, leaves Arundel looking like paper scenery. The tall Doric column surmounted by a lion ABOVE, as far from the medieval style as one can go, was erected in 1816 to the west of the castle by the Duke's tenants in gratitude for reduced rents.

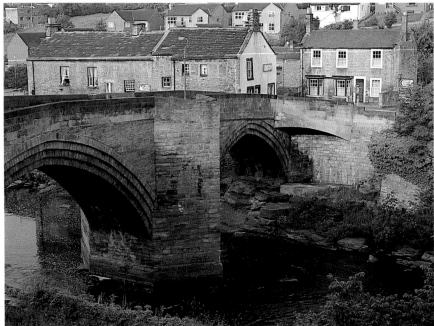

Barnard Castle

COUNTY DURHAM

The present bridge over the Tees (ABOVE, RIGHT) was built in 1569. The parapet and the shallow arches of the approach are part of improvements made after a flood in 1771. The octagonal Market Cross (ABOVE, LEFT) of 1747 has an arcade of Tuscan columns and a hall set over a lock-up that served to punish petty offenders without entirely cutting them off from society.

BARNARD CASTLE is a classic case of a town growing up beside a castle. This was founded by Guy de Bailleul in the troubled times that afflicted the north following the Norman Conquest. It has a strategic site high above the River Tees where it could guard a river crossing that goes back to Roman times. The castle was rebuilt about 1150 and the prominent Round Tower came two centuries later, so important was it to keep defences up to scratch this near the Scottish border.

The town itself shows little of these ancient military origins. Indeed the castle is remarkably invisible from the town, being hidden by houses and shops built hard against its walls and fronting The Bank, Market Place and Horsemarket. An early survivor in The Bank is Blagroves House, a Tudor mansion with a three-storeyed rectangular bay and prominent mullioned windows. It is built of the hard, pinkish Millstone Grit that gives so much of the town its character.

When peace finally came to the north after the Union of the Crowns, Barnard Castle flourished as a market town serving Teesdale, and as a weaving town specializing in yarn stockings, for which the water from the Tees was indispensable. This is evident in the Market Cross and in the long bands of windows used to light the weaving lofts of many houses built in Thorngate when weaving was a cottage industry. Later, this manufacture was taken over by mills, and many of them, now serving other industries, still stand down by the river.

The Bowes Museum (RIGHT) might look at home in Blois, but not in Barnard Castle. It was begun in 1869 by John Bowes to house the art collection that he had built up with his wife, the French actress Josephine Benôit. This explains the choice of a French architect, Jules Pellechet, and a French renaissance style. The Bank (FAR RIGHT) runs steeply downhill outside the castle walls from the Market Place towards Thorngate and the river.

The barber's shop on the LEFT faces the bustle of the Market Place. The parish church is set back from all this with a narrow opening leading from Newgate into the churchyard (BELOW), and trees to accentuate the feeling of privacy.

Beverley

HUMBERSIDE

While Hull grew into a large port, Beverley remained the county town of the East Riding and its market was fairly prosperous. It was no longer the great centre it had been, but it is nevertheless Yorkshire's most monumental small town and the most attractive. The streets around the handsome crocketed tower of St Mary's (OPPOSITE) are full of substantial 18th-century brick houses, while the stuccoed No. 11 Cross Street (BELOW), the finest early 19th-century house in Beverley, picks up the style of its porch from the giant Doric columns of the County Offices opposite.

THANKS to the Minster, Beverley looks from a distance like a medieval cathedral town. It was never that, and its origins are instead almost certainly in a monastery founded by Bishop John of Hexham, who ordained the Venerable Bede, and later came here to retire. His monastery was destroyed by the Danes, but refounded as a college by King Athelstan about 935, with a minster for its church.

The town itself grew up through the excellence of the monastery's setting. Between the chalk hills of the Wolds and the marshy carrs of Holderness, it was in an admirable position to exploit the agricultural potential of the surroundings and export its products by boat down the River Hull and over the North Sea.

So merchants and manufacturers built up the town in an easterly direction so as to be closer to the river. At the same time other traders expanded the town northwards to the present Market Place, and beyond it to the chapel of ease that later became the grand parish church of St Mary, and finally to the North Bar, rebuilt in local brick in 1409-10 (see page 14).

Textiles woven from wool brought down from the Wolds and tanning and leatherwork using the hides from the cattle of Holderness made Beverley grow to twice the size of Hull by the end of the 14th century. After that came decline. The monastic orders were suppressed at the Dissolution, and the college was disestablished in 1547, though, thankfully, the Minster was preserved. It remains today as one of the most glorious churches in the country.

THE POLITICAL CHEAP JACK

The nave of Beverley Minster (RIGHT) was started about 1308 and, by the end of the 14th century, had a lofty brick vault. This notably early use of brick is now hidden by plaster so as not to clash with the stone walls from which the vault springs. The great west window, like the rest of the west front, followed in the first half of the 15th century, and is actually higher than the nave it lights. Beneath it, the great west door is decorated with grotesques in the hollows of its mouldings (BELOW).

Just outside North Bar are the half-timbered houses designed in 1892–4 by the Beverley craftsman James Edward Elwell. He decorated them with two wooden carved panels (LEFT), taken from Punch cartoons, and two figures depicting St John the Evangelist and St John of Beverley.

Harrogate

NORTH YORKSHIRE

Betty's Café (BELOW) provides more drinkable beverages than those that Celia Fiennes drank, and a more attractive place in which to drink them. Cast iron was a favourite way to dress up a building in Victorian England, and catalogues offered numerous items ready to bolt together into porches, conservatories and verandahs. Ornate arcades, however reminiscent of draughty railway stations, only need fresh paint and some baskets of flowers to provide a welcome and a pleasant place to sit in summer.

HARROGATE is a Victorian town, yet its mineral springs were discovered in 1571. In 1598 they had already caused Harrogate to be called the English Spa, after the Belgian town, so giving the language a new word. In 1697 Celia Fiennes tried the various waters: first, 'the Sulpher or Stincking Spaw . . . its a quick purger and very good for all Scurbatick humours – I dranke a quart . . .'; second, 'the Sweete Spaw or Chalibiet', which contained iron (like the water at Tunbridge Wells); third, 'a fine cleare and sweete Spring of Common water very good to wash eyes'; and, fourth, a spring 'of a petrifying quality', which is really at Knaresborough.

It was left to the Duchy of Lancaster to develop these springs from 1840 onwards. This produced the domed Tewit Wells, St John's Well, and Pump Room, all in 1842, and the Royal Baths and Royal Bath Hospital at the end of the century. Numerous hotels came at the same time, the earlier ones classical in style, the later ones more ornate or Gothic.

People came to live here and for them were built a number of attractive terraces, notably Royal Parade, and others in Swan Road, Westmoreland Street and Crescent Road. Further out of town are individual villas that followed later in the century. Despite these developments, much common land remains, giving the town its many attractive open spaces.

The arcades of Valley Gardens (BELOW), where Celia Fiennes recorded the sulphur spa, decorate one of the swathes of green that run right into the centre of town. Glazed cast-iron arcades of a different kind protect the shops in the centre of town (RIGHT) from the worst of Harrogate's bracing climate.

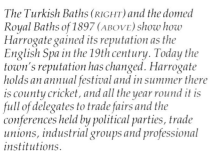

The Turkish Baths (RIGHT) and the domed Royal Baths of 1897 (ABOVE) show how Harrogate gained its reputation as the English Spa in the 19th century. Today the town's reputation has changed. Harrogate holds an annual festival and in summer there is county cricket, and all the year round it is full of delegates to trade fairs and the conferences held by political parties, trade unions, industrial groups and professional institutions.

Helmsley

NORTH YORKSHIRE

To the south-west of the town lies the castle (ABOVE). It was repaired after a three-month siege in the Civil War, but in 1689 Sir Charles Duncombe, a future Lord Mayor of London, bought it and built a new residence in the classical style half a mile away across what became Duncombe Park. The castle was left as a picturesque ruin to enliven the view.

Helmsley lies at the entrance to Ryedale between the North Yorkshire Moors and the Vale of Pickering. A short way up the dale are the ruins of Rievaulx Abbey and Byland is not far away. From their beginnings in the 12th century, these great Cistercian abbeys herded huge flocks of sheep on the moors, and over the years expanded their herds of cattle on the pastures of the river valleys as well. Because the monks wished to preserve their privacy and keep the world at a distance, Helmsley had its chance, and it rapidly became a flourishing market town dealing with the produce of the abbey's local estates. However, it never grew as large as somewhere like Glastonbury, where the abbey was within the town.

The Norman castle protected it, and a bridge across the Rye, rebuilt in 1667, led southwards out of town. The Market Place, an elongated square, became the centre of business. It is lined by all kinds of pretty houses. There is the herringbone decoration typical of 16th-century timber-framed houses in Yorkshire. There is the warm grey of the Jurassic stone that had superseded timber by the 18th century. Over all there are the red tiles made from the clays of the vale. Some buildings combine all these into an engaging mixture of materials, either by using stone for the more important parts and timber for the lesser ones, or by using timber over a stone ground floor.

The waters of Etton Gill run right through Helmsley, down the High Street and then Castlegate (RIGHT), eventually to reach the river by Rye Bridge. Beyond the roofs of the Town Hall and houses that front the High Street and Market Place is the tower of All Saints' church, built in 1866–9 in the Early English style.

In the centre of the Market Place (ABOVE), the crocketed canopy of the Feversham monument rises over the awnings of the traders. Its precise, spiky outline and pious Victorian Gothic style, the design of the architect Sir George Gilbert Scott, could hardly be further from the pedimented doorway and rough, clematis-strewn limestone walls of the Georgian house on the RIGHT, the everyday work of a local builder who knew his styles and also the local materials.

Hexham

NORTHUMBERLAND

EXHAM lies to the south of Hadrian's Wall and close to the Roman fort of Corsopitum. Some of the fort's stones were used for Hexham Priory. Yet the town owes its origin not to Rome, but to St Wilfrid, the controversial early father of the Church in England.

About 675–80, he founded a church here on land given by the Northumbrian Queen Etheldreda. Already in 681 it was the seat of a bishop, and towards the end of his life Wilfrid returned to become bishop himself. The church of those days was of a marvellous length and height, but the Danes laid it low in 876 when they sacked the town that had grown up beside it. The crypt survived and, miraculously, so did the bishop's throne, still showing scorch marks. It is the oldest article of church furniture in the country, and has a proud place in the centre of the rebuilt Priory Church.

Hexham grew up as the principal Tyneside town inland from Newcastle, with a market overlooked by two 14th-century tower houses, the Moot Hall and the nearby Prison. By their time it was not the Danes but the Scots that posed a threat to the town's security. That passed with the Union of the Crowns in 1603, and the town filled with fine houses, all built of hard Millstone Grit, which provides a good defence against the cold winds and rain of the north.

The main street of Hexham used to be Market Street (ABOVE). It and its continuation as Gilesgate take a curving path out of town from the Market Place past several pretty late 17th-century and 18th-century houses. The best are Nos. 20–22 Market Street with bay windows and pedimented doorways. In the grounds of the Priory Church there is an octagonal bandstand (RIGHT), always an occasion for a display of decorative cast-ironwork, and this supports a pretty curving roof.

St Wilfrid's church was rebuilt for a priory of Augustinian Canons betwen 1180 and 1250. The choir and transepts (OPPOSITE), exemplars of the northern Early English style of Gothic, have groups of extremely tall, narrow windows with plain pointed heads, and clusters of shafts supporting richly moulded arches, all typical of the style. The rest of the church is recent – the east wall was rebuilt in 1858 and the nave and single aisle came later still in 1907–9.

Knaresborough

NORTH YORKSHIRE

*Of the two road bridges that cross the steep
valley carved by the River Nidd, High Bridge
is essentially medieval, like the church, chapel
and castle. In spite of all this antiquity, it is
the Victorian railway viaduct (ABOVE) that
dominates the scene. It has been called a
crime, and it certainly strides across the river
in an emphatic way, but railways are now
part of England's picturesque heritage, and
this 'crime' is forgiven.*

KNARESBOROUGH rises above the River Nidd on a precipitous sandstone
cliff. After the Conquest, Serlo de Bury built a castle here, but the Scots
sacked it. It was repaired and much enlarged in the porous Magnesian
Limestone of the district in the first half of the 14th century. Then Richard II
was imprisoned here before his violent death at Pontefract in 1400. In 1644
an army of Parliamentary and Scottish troops defeated Charles I at the battle
of Marston Moor, fought close by the town, and won the north. After the
Civil War Parliament 'slighted' the castle and left it a ruin, to ensure that it
could not become a centre of renewed Royalist support.

Close by on the hillside perches the parish church, with a squat, late
medieval tower and an undersize spire. Below it is a curious chapel, primi-
tively carved into the cliffside like a miniature church.

As a market town, Knaresborough was well placed to serve both the high
moorland of the Pennines and the rich Vale of York. Wool brought some
wealth, but it was flax grown in the local fields that made the town and gave
it England's oldest surviving linen mill. Streets of houses built in the 17th
and 18th centuries distinguish the town, and so do a house of 1770 called
Fort Montague and the railway viaduct, both of them castellated in defer-
ence to the town's stirring history.

The High Street (RIGHT) is lined by stately
Georgian houses, individually built and often
with carriageways running through them to
yards at the back. Adjoining them are lower
terraces of narrow houses, and there is the
occasional house set apart from the others.
Much of Knaresborough follows this pattern.

By the entrance to the castle is the former Free
Dispensary (ABOVE) of 1853, built apart from
the other houses in a severe classical style with
a central projecting bay carrying a pediment
and uncomfortably narrow windows.

The Market Place (RIGHT) is set away from
the High Street, close by the castle, with the
classical Town Hall built in 1862. For the rest
it is full of Georgian and Victorian houses
with shops at ground level.

Richmond

NORTH YORKSHIRE

'RICHMOND town one cannot see till just upon it, being encompass'd with great high hills', wrote Celia Fiennes during her 'Great Journey' of 1698. Nevertheless it is an impressive town, built on a low hill of its own, with a castle guarding the entrance to Swaledale. It is a town remarkably in harmony with its setting, as she wrote, 'its buildings are all stone the streets are like rocks themselves . . .'

At the centre of the town, rising from the rocks, is the castle, founded in 1071, immediately after William the Conqueror had devastated the north and broken Danish power there for good. The town became the capital of the North Riding, for a while called Richmondshire. But no stirring events affected it, and, unchallenged, the great keep of the castle stands to its full height still. Sheer and gaunt, it is in stark contrast with the sumptuous Scolland's Hall, built about 1080 against the castle walls.

The Georgian houses round the Market Place set the tone for much of the rest of the town, for instance the houses in Newbiggin and Temple Square. But Richmond's most characteristic feature is the way its buildings are packed ever tighter the further up the hill they are built, to conclude with Holy Trinity church and the houses built against it to form an island in the Market before the castle, because even this open space was too valuable to remain entirely free of buildings.

The last time the Scots descended on Yorkshire was during the Jacobite uprising of 1745. Their final defeat at Culloden is commemorated by a tower just beyond the Georgian houses of Cornforth Hill (BELOW). It was built in the form of an octagon in 1746 with playful Gothick detailing, such as pointed windows, ogee arches and plaster rib-vaulting. It may not be the way to remember a bloody massacre, but it is a notably early example of this style of medieval revivalism.

The Greyfriars Café in King Street (BELOW) is a late Victorian playful mixture of 17th-century motifs that lighten the dark stone of the town and the plainer aspects of its Victorian houses and the nonconformist chapel (BOTTOM).

Immediately beneath the castle, Defoe recorded, 'there is a very large space for the Markets which are divided for the fish market flesh market and corn . . .' By 1720 there was also a market here 'for woollen or yarn stockings, which they make very coarse and ordinary, and they are sold accordingly; for the smallest sized stockings for children are here sold for eighteen pence per dozen or three half pence a pair, sometimes less'. Stocking-knitting remained a major occupation in the Dales until the end of the 19th century because it was difficult to mechanize it. It made a small contribution to the agricultural wealth that allowed Richmond to build the fine 18th-century houses that line the Market (TOP LEFT). The contrast between them, the contemporary Market Cross and Town Hall, and the view the other way from the castle (LEFT) could not be greater.

161

In the Eastern Realms

CAMBRIDGESHIRE · ESSEX
LINCOLNSHIRE · NORFOLK
NORTHAMPTONSHIRE · SUFFOLK

Essex, East Anglia and the east Midlands lay within the prosperous Roman civil zone. A drier, warmer climate than the west and generally lighter soils gave the region excellent arable land, as they still do. By the 9th century the early wealth was partly restored and now attracted the Danes. After their invasions, the east Midlands became the heartland of the Danelaw. For defence, administration and trading, the Danes founded the Five Boroughs (see page 12). Among them, Stamford remains a country town, while others such as Leicester were changed by industry.

Much of the region is low lying and the hills are modest. The flat coastal zone and the river estuaries encouraged fens that produced only rough grazing, fishing and fowling, and much poverty compared with the wealth that came from the region's arable land. Towns near the fens like Louth and Wisbech were small and far apart. In the 19th century, steam pumps ensured the long-term success of drainage schemes first introduced by the Romans and continued by the monasteries and most famously by companies of adventurers headed by Cornelis Vermuyden in the 17th century. Then the potential wealth of the fenland silt flowed in abundance. The heavy soils of the Suffolk–Essex border made excellent pasture, good streams encouraged weaving, and specialities, such as the lace-making of Nottinghamshire, gave many towns wealth from manufacturing as well as from their agricultural markets.

Essex and East Anglia have little in the way of building stone, but their clays produced oak in such abundance that this led to the rapid development of building carpentry in the 12th and 13th centuries. By the 16th century the clays were used for brick, and nowhere in the country was so quick to use it in great quantities. A band of Jurassic limestone crosses the region further north giving towns like Oundle and Stamford their honey-coloured buildings. Beyond that to the northwest the stone is variable and local clays allowed brick to come back into its own.

Aylsham

NORFOLK

Aylsham's streets of Georgian houses have comfortable red brick fronts with doorways fitting into the pattern of sash windows. This is common enough in many country towns, but often in Norfolk there are hints of the Low Countries or the Baltic in the decoration. For instance the house on the far left ABOVE has a crow-stepped gable, a feature that originated at the end of the Middle Ages in Norfolk through trade with the Baltic, and was still in use some two centuries later.

AYLSHAM is a market town by the River Bure with a large parish church and a pretty market place. The church has a lavish two-storyed porch built in 1488 and faced with knapped (i.e. split) flint. With no building stone and little timber in east Norfolk, flint was taken from the fields and gathered from the beaches to eke out supplies of stone that could be imported only at great expense.

With such poor building materials, brick was brought from the Low Countries, at first as a ballast cargo in returning wool ships. Soon immigrants from the Low Countries encouraged brick-making locally. This can first be seen at Aylsham in the Manor House, which has Tudor brickwork, though its architectural decoration is later. Shaped gables also came from the Low Countries and were used nearby at Blickling Hall about 1617–27. They entered the vocabulary of the local craftsmen who used them to decorate Bank House and The Knoll, both built after 1700.

The town is one of the most picturesque in Norfolk, and an appropriate resting place of that master of the Picturesque, the landscape designer Humphry Repton, who died in 1818. His monument carries an epitaph he composed for himself, declaiming that his mouldering remains '. . . shall give form and colour to the Rose, And while its vivid blossoms cheer Mankind, Its perfumed odours shall ascend to Heaven'.

Vegetables from Holland on sale in the Market Place (ABOVE) are no more than the latest import from a country that brought fresh ideas to Norfolk's agriculture in the 16th century. Among these were notable fallow crops like turnips and carrots. They transformed the light soils around Aylsham, *giving them an alternative to resting fallow every few years and helping to bring greater yields from the wheat harvests. The so-called Norfolk four-course rotation that they made possible may also have benefited from scarecrows (RIGHT), but this is not recorded in the history books.*

Bury St Edmunds

SUFFOLK

The two gateways are the most significant remains of the abbey. The 14th-century Great Gate has tiers of decorative niches on the outer wall, but only a single opening to enable it to withstand attack. The inner face (OPPOSITE) meanwhile has numerous shafts supporting a highly moulded arch and a large traceried window for the room in the upper storey. The abbey church rapidly became a ruin after the Dissolution, and some of its remains are now embedded in a range of houses (ABOVE).

I n Saxon times Bury St Edmunds was the capital of the East Angles and the home of a small monastery founded about 644. Their last king, Edmund, was martyred by the Danes in 869. Early in the 11th century his remains were brought to Bury, hence the town's present name. In 1020 King Canute, himself a Dane, refounded the monastery and brought twenty Benedictine monks to run it.

In 1081 William the Conqueror gave the monastery fresh privileges and Abbot Baldwin engaged on a campaign of rebuilding. This embraced the town as well, which he replanned with an extensive gridiron of streets. It is strikingly similar to the pattern used at the same time at Ludlow, though Bury lacks a castle on a cliff and instead has low town walls built on a gentle slope that runs down to the River Lark.

The town did well and money went into building it up and enlarging the monastic buildings. The Norman Gate and the Great Gate are evidence of this extended work and in their different ways combine the decorative qualities of medieval church architecture and the defensive strength of medieval castles. The Norman Gate failed to resist the riots of 1327 that followed the death of Edward II. The abbey was sacked and had to be restored, and new works included building the Great Gate.

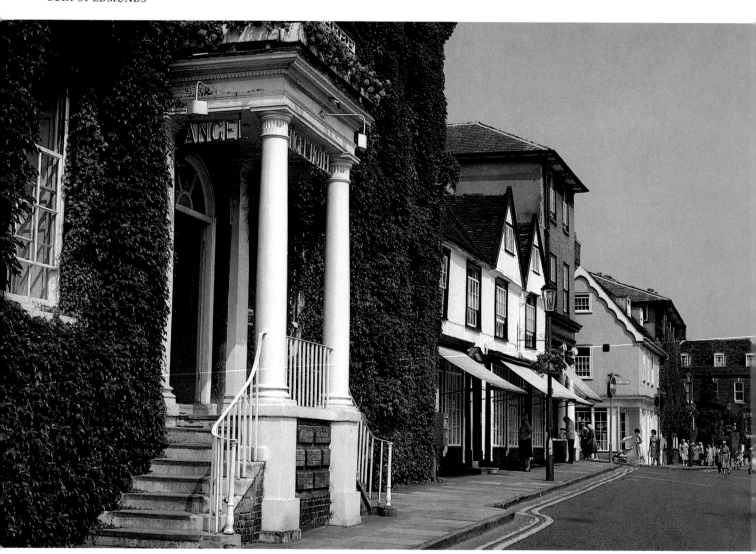

Much of the town was burnt in the riots of
1327, but it still has many timber-framed
houses, put up in the three centuries before
building in brick became cheaper and more
popular. Even so, Bury St Edmunds is
mainly a Georgian town. The Unitarian
Chapel in Churchgate Street (LEFT) was built
in red brick in 1711-12 in a robust style that
stems from the works of Christopher Wren.
The Angel Hotel of 1779 (ABOVE) faces onto
Angel Hill, the large open space at the heart of
Bury. The 19th-century Nutshell (RIGHT)
claims to be the smallest public house in
Britain, a record best tested by dropping in for
a pint.

Louth

LINCOLNSHIRE

Early wealth prompted Louth to add to the church the finest of late medieval Gothic steeples (OPPOSITE). The two tiers of openings successively emphasize the verticality of the tower, and this is taken up by the buttressing and pinnacles that rise above the junction with the tall spire. The accounts survive and they show that the steeple was built in 1501–15 at a cost of £305 7s. 5d.

Slowly the old mud and thatch houses of Louth were rebuilt in brick, and the increasing wealth of the 18th century was put into erecting many fine new houses, especially in Westgate (RIGHT, ABOVE AND BELOW). Then towards the end of the century the population of England started to rise, and with it came an increased demand for food. The town responded. The river was improved in 1770 as the Louth Navigation to give access to the mouth of the Humber so that small boats could take local produce around the coast and even abroad. Several large warehouses were built in Riverside Road to serve the riverhead for the dispatch of goods. Finally the railway arrived in 1854 with a branch line that ran up and down the county between the ports of Boston and Grimsby. Like the Louth Navigation, the railway is now a shadow of its past, but Louth still flourishes on its agricultural wealth.

Louth is a small, compact town built on a spur of the Lincolnshire Wolds, with a seemingly unplanned web of streets running down from the parish church towards the Lud, the river that gives the town its name.

Below, on the coastal saltmarshes, are the remains of the Cistercian abbey founded by Bishop Alexander of Lincoln in 1139. Louth Abbey assiduously developed cattle farming on the marshes by draining them to make lush meadows of grass. Meanwhile Louth grew rich with a market trading in the monastery's cattle and in grain that was harvested on the dry sunny chalk Wolds above the town.

In 1536 the vicar of Louth was so incensed by Henry VIII's impending suppression of the monasteries, Louth's included, that he preached the so-called 'Pilgrimage of Grace' in a vain attempt to save them. He was concerned with maintaining religious values, not trade, and it was a small affair, but it embarrassed Henry. His verbal response was to brand Louth's townsfolk 'the most brutal and beestlie of the whole realm'. Worse, he had the vicar and his supporters, including sixty citizens of the town, brought to London as rebels and hanged at Tyburn.

Thus warned, Louth retired from the margins of English political and religious history, and continued as a market town with a trade that brought increasing wealth and made it the agricultural centre of north Lincolnshire.

Oundle

NORTHAMPTONSHIRE

Cobthorne House in West Street (ABOVE) is a small version of Thorpe Hall, built near Peterborough in 1653–6 for Chief Justice St John by an associate of Wren's, the London bricklayer Peter Mills. Cobthorne House copied that building's spacious lines, overhanging eaves, perky dormers and panelled chimney-stacks, all of which remained popular locally until the end of the 17th century. The house lacks the precision that the 18th century admired, but that adds to its attractions.

'OUNDLE is a Cotswold town picked up bodily and planted on its hillock by the Nene, though we in Northamptonshire put things the other way round, and say the Cotswold towns are like Oundle and Stamford.' So wrote the local historian Tony Ireson.

True, there is a common strand in the oölitic limestone, England's finest building stone, but the undulating hills of the east Midlands are not the heaving Cotswolds and here the differences start. Unlike the west there was no heavy reliance on wool and weaving during the Middle Ages, and grain was important as it had been from at least Roman times. This gave Oundle its early wealth.

The town is first recorded in 972 when King Edgar confirmed its right to hold markets. To this day the centre of the town is the triangular Market Place with four roads leading out of it and the tall embattled tower and spire of the parish church dominating it.

Fine 17th-century houses abound, and then there is Oundle School, tucked out of the way in New Street. It was founded by Sir William Laxton, a grocer of London, in 1556 as a part of a free grammar school. When education was reformed in the middle of the 19th century, it was greatly enlarged as a public school.

Latham's Hospital, founded in 1611, the Talbot Inn in New Street, dated 1626, the White Lion in North Street (ABOVE), dated 1661, and more generally the houses in West Street make Oundle memorable for its 17th-century buildings. The Talbot Inn and the White Lion are especially notable for their projecting canted bays, a speciality of early stone houses in the Midlands. The White Lion's pair of bays rise through three storeys to end in gables and they are flanked by a pair of single-storeyed bays that continue as simple dormers in the third storey.

Contrasts in shop windows. The straight-forward windows of the butcher's shop in West Street (UPPER RIGHT) are filled with single large pieces of functional plate glass that have become traditional in the last hundred years. Meanwhile the pretty Georgian windows of the School Bookshop (LOWER RIGHT), opposite the Town Hall in the Market Place, have typically small panes of glass and heavy glazing bars. This colonnaded shop is contemporary with Cobthorne House, and has very similar sash windows in its upper storey.

Saffron Walden

ESSEX

The former Sun Inn (BELOW) shows 17th-century timber building at its most exuberant. The large windows of the Inn, visible on the right of the picture, were for status as well as for light, and the oversailing upper floors supported on jettied joists introduced an element of status again. The pargetting of the panels is content with swirling arabesques, but the gable over the carriageway (OPPOSITE, TOP LEFT) depicts the grotesque figures of the legendary Thomas Hickathrift – a local hero – and the Wisbech giant.

Essex is not part of East Anglia, though it is hard to tell its northern part from neighbouring Suffolk and Cambridgeshire. It was once wealthier than either county, and that is fully evident in the fine buildings of Saffron Walden. The Romans settled here, and the Normans built a castle, though its site had few natural advantages for defence. Nevertheless it was important since it could control a gap in the low chalk hills that run up from the Chilterns towards the Gogmagog Hills of Cambridgeshire.

In the Middle Ages wool and weaving made Saffron Walden one of Essex's most prosperous towns, but the flanking chalky fields were particularly well suited to the saffron crocus (*Crocus sativus*), whose stamens were highly prized as a dye and a medicine. So valuable was this unusual crop that the town took it for its name, and the crocus appears on its coat-of-arms (*overleaf*).

Saffron Walden has a clearly visible gridiron plan, with the huge parish church set well back from the street in a large churchyard, and the market place again set rather by itself off the main thoroughfares.

The town itself is the best place in Essex to see medieval and Tudor timber-framed shops, inns and town houses. The framing of many of them is readily visible, but others carry on the fashions of Suffolk and Cambridgeshire in having their walls thickly coated with plaster ('pargetted'), and this can then be worked up into elaborate decorative patterns.

The Eight Bells in Bridge Street (BELOW) is one of Saffron Walden's many 16th-century inns; unlike The Sun (RIGHT) it has kept its original function. The fascia that hides the jettied ends of the Eight Bells' joists is carved with leaves in a traditional way. Protected by the jetties and the roof are original bay and oriel windows, jutting out to catch the light and to provide comfortable places to sit inside.

The drinking fountain in the centre of the Market Place (FAR RIGHT) is as elaborate a reincarnation of the Middle Ages as only the Victorians could achieve, its squat columns and encrusted capitals heaped on each other in elaborate profusion.

The Town Hall in the Market Place is quite a modern building for Saffron Walden, built in 1761-2 in red brick, and ostentatiously gabled in mock timbering in 1879 in a vain attempt to give it more of the character of other buildings here. Nevertheless it would be all but indistinguishable from the brick houses nearby were it not for the prominently displayed coat of arms (TOP). The Close in the High Street is a timber-framed house with a mixture of traditional windows and a single classical one (ABOVE), which has a spider's web of leading holding in the pieces of glass.

The group of houses at the corner of Market Hill and Church Street (RIGHT) was called 'the most precious of Saffron Walden' by Sir Nikolaus Pevsner. Here one gets the clearest view of how many towns in Essex and Suffolk must have looked in the 17th century, their oversailing upper floors and jostling gables leading the eye down the street in a series of steps that seems to belie the formal planning of the town. The individuality of the houses is highlighted by the pargetting on The Sun, immediately on the right, though the less ornate houses hold their own.

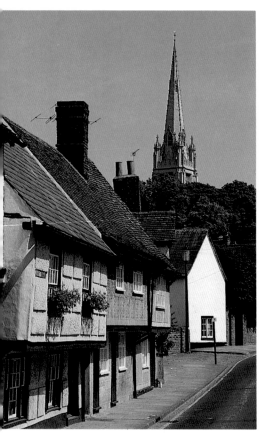

From the river at the foot of Bridge Street (ABOVE), Saffron Walden's formal planning is disguised by the rise in the street and the position of the church spire, set behind the trees and roofs of the town rather than on one of the major axes of the streets. Castle Street (RIGHT) is now a backwater of Saffron Walden, with pretty rows of small timber-framed and plastered cottages with jettied upper floors and inserted Georgian sash windows. Though the terrace came to maturity in the brick houses of the later 17th century, its origins were in earlier timber houses such as these.

Stamford

LINCOLNSHIRE

Across the river from Stamford is William Cecil's Burghley House. The Cecils, later Earls of Exeter, have their monuments in St Martin's church. The fifth Earl and his wife are remembered by an immense tomb carved in 1703 by P. E. Monnot (BELOW), showing them flanked by statues of Wisdom, visible here, and Art. Equally imposing is the Early English steeple of St Mary's church (OPPOSITE), marking the hub of the town. Once Stamford had three times as many churches, as well as a now vanished university and monastic halls.

STAMFORD stands on Ermine Street, the Roman road that leads from London to York and later became part of the Great North Road. Stamford, though, was always more than a coaching town. It started by replacing a Roman town just to the north at Great Casterton. Its strategic site on the dry north bank of the River Welland gave it direct access along the river eastwards to the fenland and westwards to the rich heartland of the east Midlands. This made it ideally suited to become one of the Five Boroughs of the Danelaw (see page 12).

As an important commercial centre it achieved renown through its fairs, but in 1461, during the Wars of the Roses, the Lancastrian army sacked the town, so little survives from beforehand apart from several churches. The town was soon rebuilt, and Browne's Hospital was erected. Stamford continued to prosper with two weekly markets as well as three annual fairs, and the inns along the Great North Road filled their courtyards with coaching traffic. When Celia Fiennes visited the town in 1697 it had become 'as fine a built town all of stone as may be seen'. Nevertheless in the 19th century Stamford stagnated. The railway passed the town by, and the Great North Road has been rerouted, but all this has ultimately been to Stamford's gain. It has kept its heritage.

Rutland Terrace (LEFT) was built in the 1820s, shortly before the town's decline. Its atttractive cast-iron balconies overlook the meadows beside the Welland. Browne's Hospital (TOP) is among the best surviving almshouses in England. It was built for ten poor men in the 1480s when the town was reviving after the Wars of the Roses. It was the gift of 'a merchant of very wonderful richnesse', William Browne, who, it is said, also paid for the steeple of one of Stamford's churches, All Saints'. The George, the most famous of Stamford's coaching inns, faces modest 18th-century shops (ABOVE), built of local stone like the houses shown above them.

Swaffham

NORFOLK

The cross (ABOVE) in the Market Place has nothing to do with commerce, but commemorates Swaffham's dead in two world wars. Monuments like this are one of the 20th century's most characteristic contributions to the ancient market places of country towns the length of England. In the background is the 15th-century church, which houses a notable parochial library of manuscripts and early printed books.

SWAFFHAM lies in the corn belt of northern Norfolk. Its old agricultural wealth is demonstrated in the parish church by a lavish false-hammerbeam roof decorated with carved wooden angels typical of the county.

Just to the west lies the Market Place, which incorporates an island formed by the Assembly Room of 1817 and the Shambles. It is nevertheless a wide open space surrounded by houses and shops. Over the top of them appears the lofty church tower carrying a thin spike-topped lantern built in 1778. It contrasts strongly with the Market Hall, built as soon after as 1783 by the Earl of Oxford. Eight Tuscan columns carry a rotunda surmounted by a figure of Ceres.

She symbolizes the increasing wealth of the county, which already for a century had benefited from the so-called Norfolk four-course system of rotation in which turnips had taken the place of fallowing to increase the yields of grain by dramatic proportions.

This greatly affected the town and its houses are pre-eminently Georgian. Apart from flint and a little building stone further west – the poor multi-coloured Greensand, locally called carstone – it was to brick that their builders turned for Swaffham's numerous fine 18th-century houses that give the town so much of its pleasantly sedate atmosphere.

The Victorians were the first to ignore traditional local materials in a wholesale way, as the rendered and slate-roofed houses overlooking the churchyard demonstrate (ABOVE). They contrast with the stabling RIGHT, built in flint with brickwork adding a splash of red to the doorways, windows and pitching-holes, a customary Norfolk combination of building materials.

Wisbech

CAMBRIDGESHIRE

Beside the churchyard is The Museum, a severe-looking house designed by the architect George Buckler and built in 1846 with a Greek Doric surround to the front door (ABOVE). Across the way is the Crescent (BELOW, RIGHT), a terrace of three-storeyed houses built rather earlier in the 19th century in a gradual curve. The Brinks are lined with ornate Georgian buildings overlooking Morton's Leam, making one of the most memorable views in all English country towns. Peckover House, built shortly before 1727, is the prize. Its classical porch and giant pilasters mark its well-proportioned front, and the back (BELOW, LEFT) has a central, pedimented doorway with a Venetian window above it and a Diocletian window – that is a semicircular window with two vertical bars – above that. The house is open to the public, so its fine interiors, including a delicate but intricately carved chimneypiece, are accessible, and so is the garden, which boasts one of the biggest maidenhair trees in England. Next door, set back, is a stable block, plain by contrast, but nevertheless handsome and still containing stalls for the horses.

WISBECH lies in the centre of the Fens, and as a port sent the produce from this rich agricultural land down the River Nene and along the coast. This brought the town some wealth, but there were difficulties: the river was meandering and shallow, and the land flooded easily. Despite many attempts to drain the Fens, it was not until reliable steam pumps arrived in the 1830s that the potential of the area could at last be fully realized.

Notwithstanding that, Wisbech owes its most memorable buildings to the influence of one man, John Morton. He supported the Lancastrian cause in the Wars of the Roses and spent some time as a refugee in the Low Countries. Here he discovered how sluggish rivers could be drained, so releasing land from the threat of flooding. On his return to England in 1485, he was enthroned as Bishop of Ely, and immediately put his experience to the benefit of his see with the construction of a new channel for the River Nene, deep and straight, called Morton's Leam. This by-passed the town of March and entered Wisbech from a new direction, so requiring embankments, which are called the Brinks. Downstream, below the lowest bridge, are the warehouses that Morton's Leam encouraged. The oldest survivor dates from the 17th century and until recently there were others from every period up to the present.

Of the two Brinks, the North Brink is decidedly the grander (RIGHT). Long rows of ambitious three-storeyed, red-brick houses give it a feeling of greater affluence than the simpler houses of the South Brink. The rows of North Brink are abruptly broken by a fine early 18th-century warehouse, its plainer front set back from the line of the houses, and punctuating their progress from the bridge.

A castle was built to the west of Wisbech church in 1072. It was demolished for a now-vanished house at the end of the 17th century, around which an attractive housing development grew up in the early 19th century. This includes the Crescent and Museum Square (BELOW), which are overlooked by the church tower.

How to Find Out about English Country Towns

THE study of towns can hardly start anywhere else but with the towns themselves. This book is no more than an introduction to the subject, so a walk round any of the towns described here will bring rewards of its own. A walk with the local guidebook ought to bring better rewards still, though guides are variable and their selection of things to see and the context in which they set them sometimes leave much to be desired. A good test is to see whether the guide starts with the town's origins and explains precisely what remains of them and where to see them.

So far as origins go, David W. Lloyd's *The Making of English Towns* (Gollancz, London, 1984) provides a comprehensive account of their evolution, with a commendable analysis of the development of town plans and a sympathetic description of the kind of buildings that filled them. Towns in the landscape are still well treated in the increasingly outdated but refreshingly written *The Making of the English Landscape,* by Professor W. G. Hoskins (Hodder and Stoughton, London, 1955 and still available as a paperback published by Penguin, Harmondsworth). M. Aston's and J. Bond's *The Landscape of Towns* (Dent, London, 1977) is a good short guide in the same vein.

The economic and geographical aspects of country towns are well covered in parts of *A New Historical Geography of England* (Cambridge University Press, Cambridge, 1973–6), edited by H. C. Darby. This has the advantage of setting the growth of towns in the overall context of England at large, but the subject needs to be extracted from a concise, dry text.

For the materials used in the building of towns, Alec Clifton-Taylor's *The Pattern of English Building* (2nd ed., Faber and Faber, London, 1972) is rightly judged a classic. Although he is weak on timber framing and by no means complete on brick, his account of stone is full of insight and a lifetime's experience. Incidentally, his books that accompanied the BBC's two 'Six English Towns' television series, *Six English Towns* and *Another Six English Towns* (BBC Publications, London, 1978 and 1984) are models of their kind. A comprehensive account of bricks and brickwork has yet to be written, but Richard Harris's little *Discovering Timber-Framed Buildings* (Shire Publications, Princes Risborough, 1978) is an absolute necessity before tackling Cecil Hewett's detailed but arcane books on the subject. For all traditional buildings, or vernacular architecture as it is called, R. W. Brunskill's numerous books, such as his *Illustrated Handbook of Vernacular Architecture* (Faber and Faber, London, and Universe Books, New York, 1971) can be relied on for clear descriptions.

There are no better compact guides to the buildings themselves than the forty-six county by county volumes of Sir Nikolaus Pevsner's *The Buildings of England* (Penguin, Harmondsworth, 1951–74), especially the later volumes and the revised editions. The series is unique for the fullness of its coverage, the excellence of its descriptions and the context in which they are set. Oddly there are no full histories of town buildings, and Pevsner's *A History of Building Types* (Thames and Hudson, London, and Princeton University Press, Princeton, 1976) is more an account of their development than a history. Even town houses lack a book of their own, though five chapters of the author's *House and Home* (BBC Publications, London, 1985) make a stab at some aspects of the subject and Sir John Summerson's *Georgian London* (Penguin, Harmondsworth and Baltimore, 1962 and later editions) has much that is applicable outside the capital. Professor Maurice Barley's *Houses and History* (Faber and Faber, London, 1986) is good for the development of house plans and perhaps the best place to read about the development of the house from its beginnings.

While some reading is indispensable to an understanding of how towns have gained their present appearance, finally the subject must be left to the individual. As a study, towns can take you in numerous directions, but the important thing is to see them and to get to know their individual characters physically. The numerous walks conducted by local historical societies and such national societies as the Royal Archaeological Institute, the Society of Architectural Historians of Great Britain, the Vernacular Architecture Group and the Victorian Society, to name a handful, can provide insight in a way that reading without looking and looking without reading never can.

If you want to become involved in the study of a town in a more positive way, the first place to start is the local history library. Here you will find what studies have previously been made and how satisfactory they are. If you want to start one yourself, you should first consult the county histories as these will give a wide range of relevant information about topography, economy, society, and history generally. Old maps will add to this by helping to build up a graphic picture of how a town has developed over the years. The statutory lists of buildings of special architectural and historic interest will describe those surviving old buildings judged by the Department of the Environment's investigators to be worthy of inclusion. Your own judgement can be sharpened on these lists, and you may well find interesting buildings that should have been included in these lists as well as the empty spaces where old buildings have recently been demolished. Whatever your findings, if you are sure of your facts it could be worth discussing them with the local council's conservation officer, though please remember that if he is any good he will be a very busy man.

The study of old buildings, finally, is a subject that could take a book of its own to explain it, but as a way of starting it is always worth looking for accounts of local buildings in the county archaeological or historical journal, and seeing what sources of information are given as references there. Manorial records, rate books, land tax assessments, hearth tax returns and leases are just a few of the documents that could help your enquiries. They take skill to use, though the local archivist might help you to interpret them. You will also discover that they will make your hands as dirty as investigating old buildings themselves. This is not a subject to undertake lightly. It can lead to addiction.

Index